T0354454

MASADA REVISITED III
and other Plays

Masada Revisited III
Irresistible Impulse
Redemption
Isaac and Amanda
One Plus One Equals One
Hypatia

ARTHUR ZIFFER

authorHOUSE®

AuthorHouse™
1663 Liberty Drive
Bloomington, IN 47403
www.authorhouse.com
Phone: 1 (800) 839-8640

Published by AuthorHouse 02/24/2015

ISBN: 978-1-4969-7077-0 (sc)
ISBN: 978-1-4969-7076-3 (hc)
ISBN: 978-1-4969-7078-7 (e)

Library of Congress Control Number: 2015902597

Print information available on the last page.

Contents

MASADA REVISITED III

A Play in Eight Scenes

by

Arthur Ziffer

Characters

Decurion

Second

Essene Woman

Essene

Woman 1

Woman 2

Woman 3

Husband of Woman 3

Eleazar ben Yair, Jewish commander at Masada

Scene 1

At rise: Sometime during 70 AD, near the end of the Jewish War (66 AD -70 AD) between Rome and the Jews living in what is today the state of Israel. A Roman Decurion and his second in command are talking after the patrol that the Decurion commands has crucified an Essene in the region between Jerusalem and the Dead Sea.

Second

Decurion, all of our men have been killed. The Jews with their bows and arrows waited until it was light and then picked us off one by one.

Decurion

Are you sure all the men are dead?

Second

Yes I'm sure, Decurion, but the man on the cross is still alive. If we leave now maybe the Jews will try to cut him down and give us a chance to escape.

Decurion

No they will kill us with their accursed bows and arrows. I should have listened to you yesterday when you said that for us to stay here and wait till the crucified man died was a mistake. We could have made it back to our lines outside Jerusalem last night and been safe.

Second

Yes, we should have just killed the man quickly instead of wasting time to crucify him; and then we could have gotten back to our lines before dawn.

Decurion

Our orders are to crucify every Jew who tries to escape from Jerusalem.

Second

But he is a skinny old man who claimed that he was an Essene and not part of the rebellion and was caught by accident in Jerusalem when the fighting started.

Decurion

Orders are orders. That's why I was promoted to Decurion and you not, because our Centurion knew that I would obey orders no matter what.

Second

And now we are going to die.

Decurion

Yes, probably, but I am not going to wait around to be picked off by some cowardly Jews with their bows and arrows. I am going to challenge whoever is out there to fight me one at a time with a sword. (He leaves.)

(After a while, Eleazar ben Yair comes up.)

Eleazar

Your Decurion was a brave man. He fought well with his sword, but he is dead. Now, if you help me get the man you have crucified off the cross, I will let you leave here and return to your legion.

Second

Yes, I will help. And the man is still alive.

Eleazar

Then I need your help in carrying him to a place where he can recuperate.

Second

You mean you are here all alone. You killed nine legionnaires all by yourself.

Eleazar

The bow and arrow can be very effective.

Second

You certainly proved that. But why are you here alone.

Eleazar

I am on my way to Masada. I am actually going to command there.

Second

Then why are you travelling alone?

Eleazar

On the way there, I wanted to see my mother; I like to be alone when I see her.

Second

But you put yourself at great risk, travelling alone.

Eleazar

Yes, but it might be the last time that I see her.

Second

I understand. By the way, my mother is Jewish.

Eleazar

What! Do you know that since your mother is Jewish that you are Jewish by Jewish law, even if your father isn't Jewish?

Second

Yes, I know.

Eleazar

The fact that you are Jewish makes me glad that it was your Decurion and not you that came out to fight me.

Second

Thank you. But I can't help but repeat how dangerous it was for you to travel alone. Look, we were ten; without your skill with the bow and arrow, you would be dead.

Eleazar

That's why we Jews use the bow and arrow.

Second

We Romans prefer the sword and to fight in formation like the Greeks. By the way, I am an expert with the sword. It would not have been as easy for you to kill me with the sword as it was to kill the Decurion.

Eleazar

Then that is another reason, besides your being Jewish, that I am glad we did not fight. But enough of this discussion; let's get the man down off the cross. There is an Essene settlement nearby. If you help me get him there quickly, he might survive.

Second

Yes, I will, but you have to let me go with you to Masada. I cannot go back to our lines alone; I would probably be executed.

Eleazar

But are you sure you want to come with me? Masada is a strong mountaintop fortress, but you Romans will certainly besiege it.

Second

I know, but at least I will have the chance to die as a Jew. I have been thinking about this for quite a while, and providence has now given me this opportunity. Furthermore, if you let me go with you to Masada, I can help the men there to improve their sword fighting skills, which I am expert at, and which will be needed against the Romans.

Eleazar

ll right, you can come with me. Let us go now.

Scene 2

At rise: A few days later. Second and an Essene woman are talking in the Essene settlement where the Essene saved by Eleazar was brought.

Second

Hello, may I take the liberty of saying that you are a very beautiful woman?

Essene Woman

You're very forward.

Second

I have been waiting for a woman like you my whole life.

Essene Woman

I am an Essene woman and you shouldn't be talking to me like that.

Second

Why not?

Essene Woman

Because it is wrong; it could lead to cohabitation which is sinful.

Second

Who says that?

Essene Woman

The elders of the Essenes.

Second

But how do the Essenes as a group survive if they don't believe in cohabitation?

Essene Woman

By adoption of orphans, and by people joining our group. Also some Essenes marry and cohabit but only to produce children, never for pleasure.

Second

Then tell me, if you don't want men to talk to you, why do you show so much of your beautiful athletic body, much more than any of the other women here do?

Essene Woman

Do I do that? I didn't realize it.

Second

I'm sure deep down in your heart that you do realize it.

Essene Woman

Alright, maybe I do realize it.

Second

Do you know why you expose yourself more than the other women here do?

Essene Woman

I don't know, but I think you think you know and are going to tell me.

Second

Maybe you are not sure you want to live a life of Essene celibacy, and you really want men to approach you.

Essene Woman

Being celibate is not my problem, but I do want to have a baby of my own to love.

Second

So do most women; it is only natural.

Essene woman

But we Essenes are supposed to resist nature.

Second

Not everybody can do that.

Essene Woman

For a Roman legionnaire, you seem very understanding about life and people.

Second

I might be a legionnaire, but I am also a person who tries to understand what life is all about.

Essene Woman

Now that we have talked a bit, I think that you are a very interesting man.

Second

Thank you. Do you know that I am going with the man I came here with, Eleazar ben Yair, who will command at Masada, to train the men there to improve their ability to fight with the sword?

Essene Woman

Yes I know.

Second

I know this is very sudden, but I don't want to be the only man there without a woman. How do you feel about marrying me and coming with me to Masada, and there together, we will produce a baby for you to love?

Essene Woman

What did you say?

Second

I have been noticing you since I've been here. As I said before, you are very beautiful; and, I think I love you. Please marry me.

Essene Woman

You don't waste any time.

Second

I know what I want.

Essene Woman

Do you have a wife back in Rome?

Second

No.

Essene Woman

Swear.

Second

I swear that I do not have a wife back in Rome or anywhere else for that matter; in fact, I have never been married.

Essene Woman

Have you had many women in your years of campaigning?

Second

No.

Essene Woman

Have you ever forced a woman?

Second

I never did. In fact, I never got promoted to Decurion, which I should have been if promotions were just based on skill and experience, because I was unable ever to bring myself to rape a female captive.

Essene Woman

Why is that?

Second

My centurion said to me, "If you can't bring yourself to rape a female captive, then you are not fit to be an officer in a Roman legion."

Essene Woman

I find that hard to believe.

Second

In fact, once in Jerusalem, a woman captive looked at me with imploring eyes, to take her and protect her from all the other legionnaires who were going to rape her. I didn't do it. I feel very guilty about that.

Essene Woman

What would happen to these women captives who were treated so?

Second

Usually they were raped by so many men that they started bleeding out through you know where.

Essene Woman

What would happen then?

Second

The women would usually die.

Essene Woman

So how would it have helped if you had taken that woman who implored you with her eyes?

Second

No other legionnaire would have come near her.

Essene Woman

Why is that?

Second

From my father, who was a legionnaire also, I learned the art of sword fighting from earliest childhood on. He was a great teacher and because of that, I was the best swordsman in my legion. No legionnaire would have dared to rape a woman that I was protecting. And by the way, my mother is Jewish, so that makes me officially Jewish.

Essene Woman

Yes it does, but what happened to the woman who implored you with her eyes?

Second

She died. I forced myself to watch from the beginning of her ordeal to the end. She kept looking at me all the time she was being violated. Was not protecting her what you Jews would call a sin of omission?

Essene Woman

I don't know, you should ask a Rabbi.

Second

If I asked several Rabbis, would they all say the same thing? You Jews are always disagreeing with each other. Do you know why Jerusalem was destroyed?

Essene Woman

Because of Roman might, I suppose.

Second

No, it was the endless fighting of you Jews with each other in the lulls between our, I mean, Roman, attacks. Jerusalem was a very strong fortress and with the water sources within the city walls, the city could have held out for years.

Essene Woman

I believe it. I see how much antagonism there is between the various groups of Jews. As an Essene, I have had much hostility directed at me by Jews of other sects.

Second

Marry me, and I will protect you.

Essene Woman

But we haven't known each other for very long.

Second

Eleazar and I will leave for Masada very soon. There is little time left before I will be gone; and, if you don't marry me now and come with me to Masada, we might never see each other again.

Essene Woman

Yes that's true.

Second

So what about it, will you marry me?

Essene Woman

Alright, I will marry you and go with you to Masada on one condition.

Second

What's the condition?

Essene Woman

That you become Jewish.

Second

But I am Jewish; by Jewish law, since my mother is Jewish, I am Jewish.

Essene Woman

I know that you are officially Jewish, but I mean I want you to start saying our prayers. You know Hebrew, obviously, since you can talk to me; it should be no problem for you to learn our prayers. And, by the way, where did you learn Hebrew?

Second

My Jewish mother made me go to Hebrew school when I was a boy.

Essene Woman

Then you must have learned the prayers there.

Second

Yes I did, and I will start saying them, now that you say you will marry me.

Essene Woman

Good. There is a Rabbi coming here in a couple of days and he can marry us.

Second

Can we start cohabiting now?

Essene Woman

No, certainly not until we are married, and then only for procreation.

Second

Were you conceived by procreation by your parents?

Essene Woman

Yes I was.

Second

Then after we are married, we can cohabit to have this baby you want so badly?

Essene Woman

All right, but remember only for procreation never for pleasure.

Second

What's wrong with pleasure?

Essene Woman

We Essenes believe that if we are doing something that gives pleasure, then we are doing something sinful. That's why, for example, we don't eat meat.

Second

I get pleasure out of eating meat and I need to eat meat to stay strong. Will you prepare it for me when we are married?

Essene Woman

Yes, but I won't eat it.

Second

That's fine with me.

Essene Woman

I think we understand each other.

Second

Another thing, what is this I hear about the people at Masada that they are mostly members of a group called "The Way"?

Essene Woman

Yes, I have heard that also; they are a strange group of Jews.

Second

Are they sometimes called Jewish Christians?

Essene Woman

Yes.

Second

There seems to be some similarity between you Essenes and the Jewish Christians.

Essene Woman

Yes, there is; both groups believe people should always do what they think is right and not what they feel like doing.

Second

What is the difference between Jewish Christians and the people just called Christians?

Essene Woman

Jewish Christians are usually Jews who have joined the group called The Way, while Christians refers mostly to pagans who have joined it.

Second

Do we have to join The Way when we get to Masada?

Essene Woman

No, I hear that all Jews are acceptable at Masada.

Second

Good, I am going to Masada to teach the Jews there how to fight Romans and not each other; although you Jews at Jerusalem, when not fighting with each other over what seems to me to be minor religious differences, fought very well against us Romans. If the Jews there could only have fought as one, we, I mean, the Romans, would never have conquered Jerusalem.

Scene 3

At rise: Some days later. The Essene who was rescued by Eleazar is talking to a woman, Woman 1, in the Essene settlement where Eleazar brought him to recover.

Essene

Thank you for taking care of me. I might not have survived without you. Not many men survive, who have been crucified, even if they are taken off the cross while still alive.

Woman 1

You were gotten off the cross soon enough and would have survived.

Essene

But you took care of me. It was several days before I could use my arms.

Woman 1

For a thin man you have very powerful arms and shoulders.

Essene

I have powerful arms and shoulders because I am a carpenter and that's probably why I stayed alive so long on the cross; I was on it for a whole night.

Woman 1

Not to change the subject too abruptly, but are you married? I heard that most Essenes do not marry.

Essene

No I am not married and you are correct; most Essenes do not marry. But you should know that; you are living here in an Essene settlement.

Woman 1

Yes, I know. But I am not an Essene. I am here by accident. I was in Jerusalem when the fighting started and I escaped. This was the first place I reached after leaving Jerusalem and now I am trapped here.

Essene

But you are alive.

Woman 1

But I don't want to be an Essene. I want to get married and have children.

Essene

Then this is not the place for you to be.

Woman 1

Yes, all the Essene men here belong to a group that doesn't marry.

Essene

Some Essenes get married.

Woman 1

But I haven't been able to convince any of the men here to marry me.

Essene

You're an attractive woman. Why hadn't you gotten married earlier?

Woman 1

In the past, when a man seemed interested in me, I would not be interested in him.

Essene

Maybe you never found anybody you really liked.

Woman 1

But I am a woman and should like a man if he likes me.

Essene

Oh, I don't think that's true. But I am not one to give advice on matters of marriage. Also, I belong to a group of Essenes that does not marry.

Woman 1

But isn't the first commandment in Scripture to "Be Fruitful and Multiply"? Doesn't that mean to get married and have children?

Essene

I am not a Rabbi. I can't answer that question, but I am sure there is an answer. Not everybody wants to get married.

Woman 1

Have you ever been attracted to a woman?

Essene

Well, yes, there were some women that I was attracted to. But I never pursued any of them; I am an Essene.

Woman 1

You said you might not have survived without me after you came down off the cross.

Essene

Yes, I did say that.

Woman 1

Then, in a sense, you owe me your life.

Essene

Yes, but then I also owe the man Eleazar my life; it was he who got me down off the cross.

Woman 1

I hear it said that you are going with Eleazar to Masada to use your skill as a carpenter to make bows and arrows for the people there.

Essene

Yes, I will go with him to Masada and make bows and arrows.

Woman 1

Then won't that be repayment enough for his saving you from the cross.

Essene

You could say that.

Woman 1

Then how will you repay me for saving you when you were recuperating after Eleazar got you down from the cross?

Essene

I don't know. What do you suggest?

Woman 1

You can marry me.

Essene

What did you say?

Woman 1

You can marry me. You owe me.

Essene

But I am an Essene.

Woman 1

Have you ever had a woman?

Essene

You shouldn't ask me that.

Woman 1

Please marry me.

Essene

What about trying to get that legionnaire, who helped Eleazar bring me here, and who will also go with him to Masada, to teach sword fighting, to marry you? It turns out that he has a Jewish mother and is therefore Jewish.

Woman 1

He has found one of the Essene women to marry him. Please marry me. I don't want to die without ever having been married.

Essene

Can I think about it?

Woman 1

No, Eleazar will leave here for Masada tomorrow morning. You have to marry me tonight. There is a Rabbi here now to marry the legionnaire and his Essene woman. He can marry us, as well.

Essene

Tonight!

Woman 1

Yes, tonight. And I promise that I will do everything in my power to make you happy.

Essene

Suppose I can't make you happy.

Woman 1

What do you mean by that?

Essene

You know what I mean.

Woman 1

Just marry me and don't worry about making me happy.

Essene

All right! I'll marry you. Let's go find that Rabbi.

Scene 4

At rise: Three years later. Three women are talking on the last night after the Romans, after building a ramp up to the mountaintop using Jewish slave labor, have finally breached the wall around Masada and will be able to enter the stronghold the next morning.

Woman 2

The high council is meeting to decide what to do when the Romans enter the compound tomorrow morning.

Woman 1

What else is there to do but just surrender?

Woman 2

A lot of the men would rather not be taken alive.

Woman 1

At least they would still live.

Woman 2

No, then they would be crucified. We have held the Romans at bay for three years and they are furious at us for holding out so long, especially with the number of them who got Leprosy from baking three years in the awful heat at the base of this mountain, while we enjoyed the relative coolness of the mountaintop.

Woman 1

Is crucifixion so much more terrible than being killed in other ways, like with a sword?

Woman 2

Yes, it is a very slow and painful way to die.

Woman 1

I didn't realize that. How so?

Woman 2

Your arms are tied to the crossbeam of the cross and your legs to the upright. When you hang by your arms, you can't breathe. Then you have to lift yourself up by your legs so you can breathe. But then your legs get tired and you have to hang by your arms and can't breathe again. This goes on and on, successively hanging by your arms and not being able to breathe and then having to lift yourself up by your legs to breathe until finally you can't lift yourself up anymore and you die, essentially of suffocation.

Woman 3

Now I understand why the Romans break the legs of somebody they have crucified if they want to speed up the dying. But it is a horrible way to die. Why are the Romans so cruel?

Woman 2

They are usually only cruel to people who rebel. And they consider our defense here at Masada as rebellion.

Woman 1

So what are the men planning to do and what about the women and children?

Woman 2

The men feel, that rather than let their children be sold as slaves to die slowly working in Roman mines and the women raped repeatedly until they are dead, that each man must put away his own wife and children first, and then a group of ten of the men will be chosen to kill all the other men, and then one of the ten chosen to kill the other nine, and then finally the last man left kills himself.

Woman 1

But isn't there a Jewish saying, "To Life."

Woman 2

Would you rather die slowly in agony or quickly?

Woman 1

I just don't want to die.

Woman 2

You might not have that choice.

Woman 1

I'd kill my husband before I'd let him kill me.

Woman 2

That doesn't sound like you love him.

Woman 1

Yes, that does sound bad; it's just that our marriage has not been a good one.

Woman 3

I think my husband would not kill me if I asked him not to, especially since we have no children.

Woman 2

(Looking at Woman 3.) You're so beautiful; you might be lucky and have a Roman officer take you for himself. But you'd have to survive the initial Roman onslaught.

Woman 3

Yes, you're right. To do that maybe I could stay with the five orphans who hide in a cave? Has the high council decided what to do with them?

Woman 2

I have the feeling the high council will not concern themselves with the orphans.

Woman 3

Then to survive the initial onslaught, I will hide in the cave where the orphans hide and come out after it is over. Also, somebody should look after them.

Woman 1

(Looking at Woman 3.) I have no children either and would also like to survive; maybe I could hide in the cave with you and the orphans.

Woman 2

(Looking at Woman 1.) You are not so beautiful as to catch the eye of a Roman officer. Would you risk being raped to death? There are so many legionnaires who have been here so long without women that they would keep raping you until you died.

Woman 3

(Looking at Woman 1.) Maybe you could avoid that. I would like to have you join me in the cave of the orphans. If we wait until the fighting is over, maybe by then the Romans would be over their initial bloodlust and not rape us.

Woman 1

(Looking at Woman 3.) And I would come out of the cave after you, when the Romans might be so transfixed by your beauty, that they would ignore me.

Woman 2

(Looking at Woman 1.) Would you run the risk of being raped to death?

Woman 1

I don't know. I have something to tell you both.

Woman 3

Some secret you have. We all have our secrets.

Woman 1

I have never been really sexually satisfied by my husband.

Woman 2

And whose fault is that?

Woman 1

My husband is an Essene and doesn't approve of sexual intercourse.

Woman 3

But not all Essenes are like that.

Woman 1

I know, but my husband is a member of an Essene group that thinks that sexual intercourse is sinful and should be done only for procreation, not for pleasure, and he behaves accordingly.

Woman 2

Than how come you married him?

Woman 1

I was getting old and men were not looking at me anymore like they used to, and I begged him to marry me and he agreed.

Woman 2

Has he tried to sexually satisfy you?

Woman 1

He has tried, but it has never worked.

Woman 2

Why is he up here in this stronghold, if he is an Essene?

Woman 1

During the fighting in Jerusalem, he tried to leave the city and was captured by a Roman patrol. They tried to crucify him, tying him to the cross to die. But our commander, Eleazar, on his way here, came upon the crucifixion, and he killed all but one of the legionnaires in the patrol; the one he spared then helped him get my husband-to-be off the cross while he was still alive. Then they brought him to this Essene settlement, where I was, to recuperate. That is when we met and got married.

Woman 3

So he is here at Masada out of gratitude for his being saved by Eleazar.

Woman 1

Yes, and he brought me here to this isolated mountaintop. I told him we should not come here, that we did not belong here. But he insisted.

Woman 3

(Looking at Woman 1.) Isn't your husband the expert at making bows and arrows?

Woman 1

Yes, he is. (Looking at Woman 3.) And, since, as you know, your husband is his chief helper, they will probably spend all night, ignoring us, making arrows in case there is any fighting tomorrow.

Woman 3

What do you mean, fighting tomorrow? What about the plan for the men to all die before the Romans come into the fortress?

Woman 2

It seems there is an alternate plan: and that is that the men would put away their wives and children quickly so they won't suffer; but then, instead of dying themselves, some of the men want to fight and kill as many Romans as they can. They feel they could make it very expensive for the Romans

Woman 3

But what about being taken alive and crucified?

Woman 2

To avoid the horrible agony of crucifixion, each man will carry a short Sicarii knife and will plunge it into his neck to kill himself if he thinks he might be taken alive.

Woman 3

It is beginning to sound like some of the men have decided, after dispatching their families, to fight rather than die according to the original plan.

Woman 1

It does sound that way.

Woman 2

I'm sure that some will fight, after having made sure that we, their wives and their children, will have a quick and merciful death and won't suffer unnecessarily; and then, make the Romans pay dearly for those lives. I know my husband.

Woman 3

How do you feel about that?

Woman 2

I trust my husband. I don't want to be raped to death by Roman legionnaires and I certainly don't want my children to die slowly as slaves in Roman mines.

Woman 1

I understand that. (Looking at Woman 3.) Since I told you my secret what is yours?

Woman 3

I don't think my husband thinks that sexual intercourse is sinful, but I have never really been able to surrender myself completely to him. I try and try but it never seems to happen.

Woman 1

Is that why you have no children?

Woman 3

Possibly, but I have known women who have never been able to surrender themselves completely to their husbands who do have children.

Woman 1

(Looking at Woman 3.) You know we are the only two women in the compound who have no children and tonight our husbands will be busy making arrows and will probably leave us to our own devices. Therefore can I presume that you and I are agreed about us hiding out with the orphans in their cave?

Woman 3

Yes.

Woman 1

Then let us go now to the cave of the orphans.

Woman 2

Goodbye my friends and know that I see nothing wrong in what you are planning to do, and God bless you both.

Woman 3

God bless you.

Woman 1

Yes, God bless you.

(They all leave.)

Scene 5

At rise: Later that night. Eleazar is addressing the defenders of Masada.

Eleazar

Tonight is our last night of freedom. Tomorrow morning the Romans will surely come through the breach in our wall. Should we surrender? You all know what will happen if we do. Your children will be sold into slavery to work the rest of, what will be, their short lives, dying slowly, bit by bit, of thirst, hunger, overwork, and beatings in Roman mines. Your wives will be raped repeatedly until they are dead by legionnaires who have been without women for three years. And you men will be crucified. We can avoid this by first doing something tonight that is very difficult, yes very difficult. And that is, that each man must dispatch, yes put away, his own wife and children. This way they will die quickly and mercifully. How could any man stand by to see his wife and children taken away from him with the prospect of a horrible death awaiting them when he could have spared them this agony? After doing this, each man will then have a choice: if his grief over having killed his wife and children is greater than his desire for revenge, then he can die with his family. But I know from what I have been hearing that some, if not most, of you will want to make the Romans pay dearly for forcing us to dispatch our loved ones. Now if a man wants to die with his family, let it be so. But for those of you, who want to take some revenge on the Romans, there is a plan to fight. Remember, we are in a good position here, are well armed, and are good fighters. We are especially good with the bow and arrow. We could kill a lot of Romans when they enter the compound tomorrow morning. With this prospect in mind, the high council has discussed what would be the best way to fight and have come up with the following plan. We start with a tight half-ring around the breach in our wall so that we can kill the Romans as they come through it and before they can get into formation. Further away, on the higher ground of one of the palace levels, will be stationed our best archers. This will include five women, who happen to be expert archers, and who have indicated that they want to fight with the men. They will be positioned there with their husbands who will be able to make sure that none of their wives will be taken alive. Furthermore, on that palace level, there will be stockpiles of swords, spears, and, of course, bows and arrows, as well as water. The most difficult part of this plan will be the retreat to the palace level when a signal is given. This signal to retreat will be given when the Romans break through our half-ring around the breach, and the retreat will be covered by our archers on the palace level. With the element of surprise, we should be able to allow a large number of our men to make it up to the palace level to continue fighting. Also, I want every man to carry a short Sicarii knife so that if he thinks he will be captured while still alive and then crucified, he can, if he wants to, kill himself. Furthermore, if an archer sees a Jew on the verge of being taken alive, I want that archer to kill him. This way we can deprive the Romans of crucifying any of our captured. We are the last stronghold of our people; and by what we do here tomorrow, we will teach the Romans what Jewish determination, or, as some say, what "Jewish Iron," is all about. So then I want you all now to go back to your huts and do what has to be done with your families, and then prepare for the Romans coming tomorrow morning. Finally, I want to give all of you the blessing of our one mighty and perfect God and thank you all for having come here to Masada. You didn't have to come here and I thank you one and all for that.

Scene 6

At rise: Second and his Essene wife are talking in their hut.

Second

You know what all the men are doing now.

Essene Woman

Yes I know.

Second

You Jews are tough. To kill one's wife and children cannot be easy.

Essene Woman

You of all people should know why it is necessary. You saw a woman raped to death.

Second

So am I supposed to kill you and our child?

Essene Woman

Yes, if you want us to die quickly and mercifully.

Second

Are you sorry you married me and came here to Masada?

Essene Woman

No.

Second

But you are going to die young.

Essene Woman

But these three years up here at Masada, having a child and living with you, have been glorious. As an Essene I never thought love could be so grand.

Second

So you love me?

Essene Woman

Yes.

Second

As much as I love you.

Essene Woman

I love you almost as much as I love our child.

Second

That's to be expected.

Essene Woman

No matter what happens, I am glad I came here with you.

Second

Thank you for saying that.

Essene Woman

Did you mind giving up meat here at Masada, which you said you love?

Second

No, I quickly got used to it, and it seems not to be necessary to eat meat to stay strong.

Essene Woman

To get to something more important than meat, you've made the men here at Masada as expert with the sword as they are with the bow and arrow. Tomorrow when the Roman break through, they are in for a surprise. You did a great thing and I am so glad to have been instrumental in helping you do this by making it easy for you to come to Masada.

Second

Yes, you made it easy for me to live here, but I must say that you Jews were apt pupils.

Essene Woman

Don't say you Jews. You are as much a Jew as anybody here. Your mother is Jewish, so you are officially Jewish. But more than that, you live as a Jew, and therefore you are Jewish if you want to be.

Second

Thank you for saying that. But tell me, why are we up here? Why did the people here allow themselves to be trapped up here on this mountaintop?

Essene Woman

I've wondered about that myself.

Second

And also who is that old man living with his family apart from the rest of us in one of the palaces who keep to themselves? I have a feeling that everyone is here to protect him.

Essene Woman

Since we are not members of The Way, none of the other people here at Masada would ever tell me anything about him, except that he was an important person in The Way, somehow connected with the founding of the movement, and that he was crucified way back when but by some convoluted plot survived the cross.

Second

Should we have become members of The Way?

Essene Woman

It wouldn't make any difference now.

Second

Don't you want to know what we are going to die for?

Essene Woman

It would help, but we are still going to die.

Second

You know, I have an idea on how we can survive.

Essene Woman

Oh, why don't you tell me?

Second

You, I, and our child, go down the Snake Path which the Romans don't guard, since it is so difficult a descent, and then make it to the camp of the Jewish slaves that built the ramp up to here, hopefully unnoticed by the Romans.

Essene Woman

And then what?

Second

After Masada is taken, the Romans will probably just disband the slave camp, since the slaves there were not involved in any rebellious activities, and let them fend for themselves; and then we can go to some Essene village.

Essene Woman

Would we go down the Snake Path by ourselves?

Second

Yes.

Essene Woman

Why can't we take others with us?

Second

Firstly, only a small group, namely, we three, with me carrying our child, could do it without making noise and attracting the attention of the Romans; and, secondly, of all the women in the compound, very few have your physical capability to climb down the difficult Snake Path; and, finally, the people here are mostly members of The Way and would not leave Eleazar and that secretive old man they might be here to protect.

Essene Woman

When would we go?

Second

Soon; in fact, we should go shortly after I say goodbye to a few people.

Essene Woman

What happens if we are caught by the Romans?

Second

You know what will happen. Are you willing to risk it?

Essene Woman

Yes.

Second

Then let us prepare to go.

Scene 7

At rise: Still later that night. The Essene and the husband of Woman 3 are talking.

Essene

Well, we are finished with what we had to do. We have distributed all the arrows we made and have built ourselves a little perch on the highest level of this palace where we can look down on everybody. We should be able to kill a lot of Romans from here.

Husband

This is a good idea. We can shoot our long bows from here and very few Romans will be able to shoot back. Now, not to change the subject, should we worry about our wives?

Essene

No. They know where we are and would come to us if they wanted to. But I am still worried about the five orphans. Are we doing the right thing by ignoring them?

Husband

Did you speak to Eleazar about them?

Essene

Yes I did, and he said that the high council had decided that only parents of children have the right to kill them, so the orphans will not be dispatched like the other children.

Husband

Maybe our two wives, who have seemed to disappear, will take care of them.

Essene

Yes, I think I overheard some talk about them staying in the cave where the orphans hide out.

Husband

Good. I would hate for the orphans to just be ignored.

Essene

But let us talk about what is going to happen tomorrow morning. The Romans will enter the compound, probably at dawn. With our long bows we should be able to kill anyone coming through the breach. We should especially try to kill any officers who we see and also anyone wearing a vest, since our arrows fired from a long bow can pierce a vest.

Husband

Not to change the subject again, it is interesting that we two are up here together: both of us have no children and it seems that neither of us will kill his wife.

Essene

Yes that is interesting.

Husband

Do you have any doubts about us killing Romans? It does say in Scripture, "Thou Shalt not Kill."

Essene

I have no problem with killing Romans. They could just ignore us on this mountaintop. We are no threat to them. Also Scripture says that killing is allowable under certain circumstances. Certainly, self-defense is one of the circumstances.

Husband

How do you feel about suicide in order to avoid being taken alive and crucified?

Essene

I have no problem with that. Crucifixion is a horrible way to die and, as you know, I was almost killed by crucifixion three years ago.

Husband

You know that I am a Jewish Christian and, to some of us, suicide is considered a sin.

Essene

If you want, I can try to kill you and not let the Romans take you alive.

Husband

Yes I'd like that, if it is at all possible.

Essene

You know, part of our mission up here is to make sure that no Jew is taken alive. That means if we see that a Jew is going to be captured while still alive then we should try to kill him. Are you going to be able to do that?

Husband

Yes although, I would find it easier to kill Romans.

Essene

I'll tell you what: you focus on killing Romans and I'll worry about killing captured Jews.

Husband

Thank you. Do you wonder if, even though that legionnaire whom Eleazar brought with him and who has spent the last three years training our men in the niceties of swordplay, our men will do well in actual sword combat?

Essene

Yes. I think the Romans will find that we are as good with the sword as they are. By the way, did you hear that the legionnaire will leave the compound later tonight with his wife and child and go down the Snake Path hoping, with his knowledge of a Roman camp, to get to the camp of the Jewish slaves, whom the Romans used to build the ramp up to here, to hide away in that camp and possibly stand a good chance of surviving?

Husband

Yes, I have heard that, but if he is captured he will be crucified.

Essene

Yes, but he says that he will make it costly for the Romans as long as he has his sword.

Husband

He is a good man and I hope his plan works. By the way, do you find it interesting that our two wives have become so close?

Essene

It was to be expected since they are the only women up here who have no children.

Husband

I have a confession to make.

Essene

You don't have to confess to me.

Husband

I want to.

Essene

All right go ahead.

Husband

I could never really make my wife happy sexually.

Essene

Maybe it wasn't your fault.

Husband

Yes. She married me too quickly. She was very anxious to get out of her parent's house. Her mother couldn't wait for her to get married and leave.

Essene

Do you know why?

Husband

I think it was because her father couldn't stop staring at her, probably because she is so beautiful; and that made his wife, her mother, very angry. She, my wife-to-be, realized this and she married at her first opportunity, which turned out to be me, to get out of her parent's house.

Essene

But you are so well-matched. She is one of the most beautiful women in the compound and you're a very handsome man, if I can say that without embarrassing you.

Husband

Are you saying she married me because of my appearance, and that she really didn't love me?

Essene

Appearance is very important. Our first king, Saul, was chosen because of his appearance.

Husband

But he turned out to not be a very good king.

Essene

That's true.

Husband

You know it bothered me when you said that I am a very handsome man.

Essene

I'm sorry but you are. I have a confession to make also. Like your wife, my wife has not been happy sexually with me. But it is my fault, not hers.

Husband

Why is that?

Essene

I never had strong feelings for her.

Husband

You know that sometimes I notice you staring at me in a very strange way?

Essene

Yes, I'm sorry about that too.

Husband

Is this occasional staring at me one of the reasons why you chose me as your chief helper?

Essene

Yes, but you have proved to be very adept at making bows and arrows, and furthermore, you have become the best long bowman in the compound.

Husband

You taught me well.

Essene

I appreciate your saying that.

Husband

Since tonight might be our last night alive, do you want to discuss further your reason for staring at me occasionally?

Essene

Yes and no, but more "no" than "yes."

Husband

I understand. By the way, does it bother you that some Jews feel, since neither of us has any children, that we have violated the law in Scripture "Be Fruitful and Multiply"?

Essene

I've thought about that; and I think I have an answer. Namely, God tries to communicate with man, and man writes down in Scripture what he thinks God is telling him. But the words of Scripture are only man's approximation of what he thinks God is saying. Isn't it presumptuous of man to feel that his choice of words for what God is saying are the ones that God would choose? Now as far as being fruitful, we have been fruitful. We have been fruitful in that we have produced for Eleazar and all the people up here at Masada, the best possible bows and arrows. Also, as far as multiply is concerned, I have multiplied by training you. And if you survive tomorrow, you will multiply by training your helper, like I have trained you.

Husband

Thank you for explaining that to me.

Essene

It is getting very late. Let us eat and drink and rest a little, so we can do what Eleazar wants us to do when the Romans come through the breach tomorrow.

Husband

Yes we should. I want to thank you for all the time you spent training me.

Essene

As a student, you might have outdone your teacher. And you are certainly better with the long bow than I am.

Husband

Thank you. And God bless you.

Essene

And God bless you.

Scene 8

At Rise: A few months after the fall of Masada, Second and his wife, the Essene Woman, are living in an Essene village near the Dead Sea.

Essene Woman

I feel guilty that we went down the Snake Path ourselves and did not save anybody else from Masada. Every Jew there died except for five orphans and two women who hid in a cave during the fighting and two men and Eleazar who were captured alive.

Second

We had no choice.

Essene Woman

I know but I still feel guilty.

Second

You Jews feel guilty about everything.

Essene Woman

I told you not to talk like that; you are as Jewish as any other Jew. Because you said that I am not going to cohabit with you tonight.

Second

But we are trying to get you pregnant again.

Essene Woman

We can skip tonight. Besides the people here stare at me as if I am doing something wrong by cohabiting with you so frequently; it seems in a small village like this, everybody knows everybody's business.

Second

No, the women stare at you because they are jealous of your beauty, and the men stare at you because they all want you, even if they are Essenes.

Essene Woman

You're probably right but I want to leave this village and go to a bigger one, or a city even, where we can avoid the pettiness of a small village.

Second

I am ready to go whenever you are. But your mention of the word "city" brings up something that I have been meaning to talk to you about.

Essene Woman

And what is that?

Second

I can't get over how the people at Masada behaved compared to the way the Jews of Rome, where I grew up, would have behaved if they had faced the same situation as the Jews at Masada did when the Romans were ready to break through.

Essene Woman

What do you mean?

Second

You know that even though my father was not Jewish, all our family friends were Jewish, which was my mother's doing, although my father didn't seem to mind.

Essene Woman

Was your father accepted by your mother's friends?

Second

At first not so much but after a while any objection to him seemed to disappear.

Essene Woman

Do you know why?

Second

Well for one, he was a very good man.

Essene Woman

And is there a second reason?

Second

Yes, he not only taught me the art of sword fighting, but any Jewish boy in the community who wanted to learn. Most of the parents of these boys were grateful for this.

Essene Woman

You were talking about the difference between the Jews at Masada and the ones in Rome.

Second

Yes. Most of the Jewish men I knew in Rome did not seem to be like the men at Masada, who were fighters. The Jewish men in Rome were not fighters but merchants and tradesmen.

Essene Woman

Like some of the men in the big villages and cities here in Judaea.

Second

Yes, but more importantly, most of the wives of these men did not seem like they would allow their husbands to put them and their children away like at Masada.

Essene Woman

You mean even if they knew the alternative was a horrible death.

Second

They probably would not have allowed themselves to think of that.

Essene Woman

You know, even at Masada, a lot of the women had to be convinced by other women what was in store for them if their husbands did not put them away.

Second

So are the Jews of Rome different than the ones at Masada.

Essene Woman

The differences may be superficial. You notice how good Jewish men are as merchants and tradesmen. There is a saying in Scripture: "Whatever your hand finds to do, do it with all your might."

Second

Maybe that's why the Jewish community accepted my father, because he was so good as a sword fighter.

Essene Woman

The scriptural command to do what one does with all one's might, which made Jewish men so good in being merchants and tradesmen, would have transformed them into their doing what had to be done at Masada. Remember some of the people at Masada were merchants and tradesmen before they went to Masada.

Second

I don't see the connection.

Essene Woman

It is hard to explain.

Second

And what about the wives of these Jewish merchants and tradesmen? It seemed to me that to many of the Jewish wives of Rome, the idea of being put away by their husbands would be unthinkable. I cannot imagine many of them accepting this. In fact, I think some would have been so resistant to the idea of being put away by their husbands that they would have not allowed it.

Essene Woman

The wives accepted it at Masada; and, the Roman Jewish wives would have accepted it also when they finally realized it was the best possible option.

Second

I am glad that we escaped from Masada and I did not have to put you and our child away.

Essene Woman

So am I.

Second

I'm also glad that you had the physical ability to climb down the Snake Path and the courage to risk being caught alive by the Romans, much as I would have tried to prevent that.

Essene Woman

There is an old saying that It takes three things to live the good life: courage, God's grace, and knowledge; but, unfortunately, you need them in that order.

Second

That's interesting and I certainly agree with that.

Essene Woman

Maybe we can cohabit tonight.

Second

Okay. But I am a little tired now.

Essene Woman

You're playing with me now, but I guess I deserve it.

Second

No, you don't deserve it. You have done so much for me that you would never deserve my playing with you for real. Besides your loving me, I will be eternally grateful to you for having made it easy for me to go to Masada; and there, become part of the fighting heart of Israel. This is true even though I did not do any fighting, which by the way I feel guilty about. I would have liked to have fought with the men I trained.

Essene Woman

Now you are having guilt feelings; that proves you are Jewish.

Second

Now you are playing with me.

Essene Woman

I am sorry. But in a sense, you did fight at Masada but it was vicariously. It has been reported that over a thousand Roman legionnaires died at Masada, many of them by Jewish swords. Every Roman that died by a Jewish sword was partly your doing.

Second

Thank you for saying that. But I still would have liked to have actually fought with the men.

Essene Woman

You were not obliged to fight. We were not members of The Way like most of the others who were there to protect Eleazar and possibly that secretive old man and his family who stayed by themselves in one of the palaces. Besides, if you had fight at Masada, I and our child would not be alive now.

Second

All right, I'll go along with that.

Essene Woman

You know maybe it is time for us to go to bed.

Second

Yes maybe it is.

(Curtain.)

IRRESISTIBLE IMPULSE

A Two Act Play

by

Arthur Ziffer

Characters

First Detective

Second Detective

Therapist

Girlfriend of Victim

Man/Defendant

Prosecutor

Defense Attorney

Therapist for the State

Act I
Scene 1

At Rise: Girlfriend of a therapist who was killed and the man who killed him are talking in girlfriend's apartment.

Girlfriend

(Hollering at man.) You killed my date. You hit him with a pipe. You killed him.

Man

Please don't scream at me.

Girlfriend

You followed me home. Why?

Man

I couldn't resist.

Girlfriend

Are you going to kill me too? I am the only witness to the killing.

Man

No.

Girlfriend

God, this is a strange conversation.

Man

Yes it is.

Girlfriend

I am not afraid of you.

Man

I am glad, because I have no intention of hurting you.

Girlfriend

So why did you follow me home.

Man

Because you are such a beautiful woman. Also I was curious why you left after you bent down and touched your date's neck? Although I guess you were seeing if he was dead.

Girlfriend

Yes, once I saw that he was dead and I could do nothing for him, I left because I didn't want to get involved.

Man

You are involved. Sooner or later the police are going to find out that you were out with him tonight.

Girlfriend

Oh my God!

Man

You touched his throat to check his pulse. Are you a medical person?

Girlfriend

I am a nurse practitioner.

Man

Is that like a physician's assistant?

Girlfriend

Sort of, similar amount of training, but a little different.

Man

You are so beautiful; I would have thought that you were a dancer.

Girlfriend

I did study ballet from the age of four till I graduated from high school.

Man

Why did you become a nurse instead of a professional dancer?

Girlfriend

There are too many dancers; it is very competitive. But why are we making small talk? You have just killed somebody. You killed my date.

Man

God, I can't believe I did that.

Girlfriend

You mean you don't know why you killed him?

Man

I don't know exactly. I saw him leave the theater with you and I lost it. What did you see in him?

Girlfriend

He was tall, good looking, and a doctor.

Man

Did you know that he thought of himself as the reincarnation of Freud? Like Freud he was a neurologist who became a therapist. Only in his case the word "fraud" with an "a" not "Freud" with an "e" should be used.

Girlfriend

Very clever, but how did you know him?

Man

He was my therapist for several years.

Girlfriend

And?

Man

He was not very good as a therapist and hurt me very much.

Girlfriend

Does that justify killing him? There are lots of doctors who have patients who feel that their doctors were no good. That's why doctors have malpractice insurance.

Man

But this was much worse than malpractice.

Girlfriend

How much worse could it have been?

Man

He made it impossible for me to get or have a woman.

Girlfriend

You mean he castrated you.

Man

In a sense!

Girlfriend

What do you mean? He certainly didn't cut off your genitals.

Man

Not physically, but emotionally.

Girlfriend

Can you explain that?

Man

According to another therapist I went to, it seems that he did something to me in the therapy that implanted into me, or at least intensified it, an inability to approach women, especially if they appeal to me.

Girlfriend

How could he do that?

Man

I not sure I can explain it.

Girlfriend

Try.

Man

The second therapist called it "countertransference."

Girlfriend

Don't you mean transference?

Man

No, transference refers to a patient transferring feelings onto the therapist. "Countertransference" is where the therapist transfers feelings onto the patient.

Girlfriend

I know that transference is very common in therapy. Is "countertransference" also common?

Man

It seems that it is.

Girlfriend

I've read that transference is supposed to be necessary in any effective talk therapy. Is "countertransference" also necessary?

Man

Not only is it not necessary, but it can be very harmful to the patient.

Girlfriend

Can you explain that?

Man

In my case, the therapist and I argued over a woman for years.

Girlfriend

What! Can you explain that?

Man

There was this woman at work, who I liked, who seemed to give me, after much back and forth, an opening to approach her and I froze and did nothing.

Girlfriend

So! Don't a lot of men do that?

Man

Probably, but after a few days when I realized what I had done and started bemoaning about my inability to have responded to the woman, my therapist claimed she did not give me an opening and therefore I did not freeze, since there was nothing to freeze about.

Girlfriend

Could he have been right?

Man

Of course, but I still should have checked the situation out; and maybe he should have pointed out to me that I should do so, or at least be aware that I was not doing so.

Girlfriend

Don't some therapists feel that they should not intervene in things like that? But why would he feel that nothing had happened? He wasn't there when the incident occurred.

Man

Exactly

Girlfriend

So how does the "countertransference" fit in?

Man

I guess unconsciously he felt guilty about not making me aware of what I had done, because of inattention or maybe he felt guilty over not wanting me getting something out of life that he never could get (Therapists want the best for their patients but something better for themselves.) and that made him angry at me (subconsciously of course). We argued over this for years.

Girlfriend

From my few dates with him, I could tell that he was the kind of person that would find it difficult to admit that he had made a mistake. But how did that make it impossible for you to approach women?

Man

As a second therapist explained it to me, the so-called oedipal triangle from the Oedipus complex - with the first therapist playing the role of a disapproving father, the woman playing the role of the mother role, and me the son - was intensified no end.

Girlfriend

Isn't the Oedipus complex about a man wanting to sleep with his mother?

Man

That's an oversimplification; a man wants to sleep with a suitable substitute for the mother. I'm sure you've heard the song that begins, "I want a girl just like the girl that married dear old dad."

Girlfriend

How can you conflate that hokey song with the Oedipus complex?

Man

I don't think I can explain the complications of the Oedipus complex to you.

Girlfriend

Can't a man just meet a woman and there be no other man involved?

Man

Yes, if the man has resolved the basic Freudian mishmash of the oedipal triangle. However, a lot of men seem to reach adulthood with an unresolved oedipal fixation which leads to various problems. One of the manifestations of this is that I have known many men who if they see me with a woman, and if for some reason they feel threatened by me, will say to me that they desperately want to meet her; but I'm sure that if they had not seen her with me they would not have had the slightest interest in the woman. Many times when this happens and I introduce them to the woman, they go out with her once, and then lose interest in her if they think I am not interested in her.

Girlfriend

Yes, I know what you mean, but what kind of problems did it cause for you?

Man

Well, inability to approach a woman who appeals to me, for one.

Girlfriend

But that's very common, what else?

Man

Well, impotence and/or being non-orgastic for another, both of which afflict me.

Girlfriend

I don't know why I am telling you this, but I happen to be frigid; I have never had an orgasm with a man. I guess that means that I am, what was that word you used, non-orgastic?

Man

But you're so beautiful.

Girlfriend

Can't a good looking woman be frigid?

Man

That surely is one of nature's biggest jokes.

Girlfriend

In fact, I was going to break off the relationship with the doctor tonight. This always happens; I have never had an orgasm with any man that I've dated and always end up breaking up with them. Also, he really wasn't a very nice person.

Man

Do you know why you are frigid or, as you put it, can't have an orgasm?

Girlfriend

Unfortunately, when I was a kid my mother used to say to me that a man could do things to a woman that were so bad that the woman would rather that the man had killed her.

Man

That's terrible!

Girlfriend

Yes, but your killing my date was worse.

Man

I don't understand how that happened. I can't believe I did such a thing. Pick up a pipe and hit him on the head.

Girlfriend

But it did happen.

Man

Do you remember saying to me that if I didn't kill you, you would never identify me?

Girlfriend

Yes, at that moment, I was afraid of you.

Man

But you are not afraid of me now?

Girlfriend

No. By the way, you keep saying that I am so beautiful. Did that have anything to do with your killing my date?

Man

Maybe, the idea of him having a woman that looks like you, rather than me having you, just galled me.

Girlfriend

I suppose that is flattering. But to get back to your therapy, you said that you and the therapist argued for years over a woman. Why didn't you just quit the therapy?

Man

That's a good question. If you have never been to therapy it would be hard to explain.

Girlfriend

I have been in therapy, in fact, many therapies with different therapists, and it never seemed to help; but I have never had a problem quitting if the therapy didn't seem to be helping. What's it like to argue for years over a woman?

Man

The time goes by endlessly with the therapist just whipping you verbally with flip remarks like "What do you think?" or "Why do you ask?" and avoiding coming to grips with the incident where I, supposedly, froze up with the woman at work and he denying that it happened. You get angrier and angrier. Finally you begin to express the anger.

Girlfriend

Maybe that was the point of the therapy. Despite the fact that you killed somebody tonight, and I can't believe that I

---

am saying this, but you do seem to be the kind of person that never gets angry, even when you should.

Man

You're not the first person to say that to me.

Girlfriend

So why do you feel that he was not doing his job; maybe his job was to get you so angry that you would express it?

Man

It was the way he ended the therapy.

Girlfriend

How was that?

Man

As I said, I was getting angrier and angrier and I started cursing and screaming. I started doing it when I was by myself. The problem was that I could not do it in the therapist's office.

Girlfriend

You mean, you would curse and scream when you were alone in your apartment.

Man

Yes, and in my car too which is a better place than in the apartment. When I did it in my apartment, my neighbors could hear me and must have thought I was crazy. In the car nobody can hear you as long as the windows are closed, although once a co-worker drove by me and saw me gesticulating out of anger very vigorously by myself. He asked me about it at work the next day; I mollified him by saying that he caught me with a case of the "screamies." He was a "savvy" kind of guy and understood.

Girlfriend

Boy, the therapist really did a number on you

Man

Gee, most people would say that I was so angry because I had transferred anger toward someone else, like my mother, onto him.

Girlfriend

Do you think that is a possibility?

Man

I guess it's possible; I did have problems with my mother. But I just felt that the therapist was messing with me.

Girlfriend

You mean consciously.

Man

Oh, maybe not consciously, but at some point he could have or should have checked out the situation with another analyst. I don't think he ever did.

Girlfriend

Okay, go on.

Man

Eventually I was able to reach the point where one day I cursed and screamed at him in as loud and angry a voice in his office as I was doing when I was alone.

Girlfriend

How did he react?

Man

He said we would have to end if I was going to do this again. Unbelievably, I said, "Okay let's end." And I unilaterally picked an ending date, about two weeks in the future, even though I had trepidations about letting the therapist precipitate an abrupt ending of the therapy. I had been going to him for six years.

Girlfriend

What happened when the day to end came?

Man

I expected him to say, "It was about time that I let him have it, and now we can really begin therapy." But all he said was that he had only been kidding (about ending the therapy if I didn't quiet down), and he said it in a very matter-of-fact way. I felt this was unconscionable, and I followed through on quitting.

Girlfriend

I think you did the right thing. You had to quit, if you could, after what he said.

Man

What was worse was that at the end of the appointed last session, he begged me to come one more time, which I did, and yet he still did not say anything that I felt he should say, although he seemed very upset, so I continued on with the abrupt ending. I guess I must seem very unforgiving to you.

Girlfriend

Did you feel that you made a mistake in coming that one last time, that maybe you let him fuck over you one more time?

Man

Somebody once said to me that I give everybody the benefit of the doubt and most of the time they don't deserve it.

Girlfriend

I'll say. If you had ended when you said you would, you might not have ended up killing him.

Man

I know.

Girlfriend

On that extra day, did you at least scream at him when he didn't say what you wanted him to say?

Man

No!

Girlfriend

That might have discharged enough anger so that you might not have ended up killing him.

Man

What a pushover I was.

Girlfriend

I hope you didn't shake his hand when you left.

Man

I don't think so.

Girlfriend

I'll bet. The trouble with people like you is that you expect a therapist to know what's happening during the therapy.

Man

Yes, I guess I did.

Girlfriend

You know, not to change the subject too abruptly, here I am talking, in a very matter-of-fact way, with the man that killed my date tonight.

Man

Oh God. I still can't believe I did it.

Girlfriend

You know it just occurred to me that I am in serious trouble.

Man

You mean because you left the scene of the crime without reporting it.

Girlfriend

Yes, but also because of your coming here and my letting you in.

Man

Why did you let me in?

Girlfriend

I am not sure, but you don't scare me; and, there is something about you that touches me.

Man

Do you like me?

Girlfriend

Let's not go into that. Let's get back to the reason why you killed my date. To a lot of people, the term "countertransference" sounds like so much "psychobabble."

Man

Yes, I know.

Girlfriend

Maybe there is another reason why you have problems with women.

Man

Well, like your childhood, my childhood was not perfect.

Girlfriend

Is anybody's?

Man

That's an interesting remark coming from a woman who might be frigid because of things her mother said to her. Are many women frigid?

Girlfriend

Probably more than you think: that's why so many women joke about faking having an orgasm. And why do you think there is such a high divorce rate?

Man

Are you saying that a lot of frigid women blame their frigidity on the choice of husband, and hope that with a different man they will not be frigid?

Girlfriend

I'm sure that happens.

Man

Does that usually work?

Girlfriend

I have friends who were frigid with one man and not with another.

Man

But you have never found a man who you were not frigid with.

Girlfriend

There was one man where I was only partially frigid.

Man

What happened?

Girlfriend

He dumped me.

Man

Why would a man break off with a woman that looks like you?

Girlfriend

He said I was a bitch.

Man

Are you?

Girlfriend

Sometimes, without realizing it, but one of my therapists said that my bitchiness with that guy was the result of some "orgasm anxiety" that I was feeling when I was with him.

Man

Not to try to psychoanalyze you, but tell me about your father.

Girlfriend

He was a very nice, gentle person. In fact he was sort of like you.

Man

But he let your mother say things to you that she shouldn't have.

Girlfriend

A man has to work. He can't be around all day, watching his wife and child. Besides that, even when he was around, my mother still said terrible things, and he would mostly do nothing.

Man

Do you blame your father at all for your problem?

Girlfriend

I do, but what good does that do? He loved my mother; she "rang his bell" so to speak.

Man

But nobody's ever "rung your bell."

Girlfriend

With your sexual problems, I don't think you should be talking about having one's "bell rung."

Man

You can be bitchy.

Girlfriend

I'm sorry, but let's get back to you. You said your childhood was not perfect. Is it possible that your problems with women were caused by your less than perfect childhood?

Man

Of course!

Girlfriend

So maybe it wasn't the therapist's fault.

Man

He didn't help.

Girlfriend

Were your parent's as less than perfect as mine?

Man

Maybe!

Girlfriend

What did they do that was so bad?

Man

Well for one, I had asthma as a teenager and when I would have an asthma attack, my mother would not call a doctor right away.

Girlfriend

Why not?

Man

When my mother was a little girl, she once had an earache and her mother wouldn't call the doctor until the neighbors forced her to, because my mother was screaming so loud.

Girlfriend

Was there a reason for that?

Man

My grandmother was a poor widow and did not want to spend the money on a doctor.

Girlfriend

Did your mother not call a doctor when you had an asthma attack for the same reason?

Man

No, we were not that poor.

Girlfriend

So what happened when you had an asthma attack, did they go away by themselves?

Man

No, my mother would relent after a few days, and call the doctor. The doctor would come and give me an injection of adrenalin, which was the usual treatment in those days. But then my mother would say that the doctor just put water into my veins and that the asthma attack was only in my mind.

Girlfriend

By saying that your asthma attack was only in your mind, did your mother mean that the attack was imaginary based on hypochondria, or that it was real but psychosomatically induced?

Man

She meant that it was imaginary, although she did see me gasping for breath. I guess she was in denial, her own history overpowering her sense of reality.

Girlfriend

What about your father during these situations?

Man

I get the impression he was like your father, and let the mother rule the roost.

Girlfriend

Could these asthma attacks have anything to do with your sexual problems with women?

Man

Well I did develop having masochistic fantasies in order to get through long nights with a full blown asthma attacks.

Girlfriend

How does that work?

Man

As my other therapist indicated, because my mother would let me suffer, I wanted to hate her, but I couldn't. It seems that I had a choice: hate my mother or myself. I mean, who can hate their mother, so I ended up hating myself and developing the masochistic fantasies. They seemed to help me get through the long sleepless nights gasping for breath when I had asthma attacks. Eventually, I outgrew the asthma, but the masochistic fantasies have stayed with me my whole life. I find them very embarrassing. This was exacerbated by a very bad experience acting in a play with a director who used his position to brutalize me and where I just let it happen and maybe even had provoked it. It resulted in my cursing and screaming when by myself, like I did when I was in therapy. I blame this partly on my first therapist, your date, the man I killed, who abruptly precipitated the ending of my therapy and left me not exactly expert in dealing with aggression

Girlfriend

Yes, I understand; I have known men with masochistic problems. But more important, is there any chance that your problems with women are that, because of the way your mother treated you when you had asthma attacks, a part of you, deep down, hates her and this has spread, through negative transference, to unconsciously hating all women? I am a nurse, and I have a lot of experience with asthma. An asthma attack can be very painful. People die from asthma attacks. Your mother not calling the doctor right away when you were having an attack was very cruel, especially since an adrenalin injection by the doctor would have cured the attack immediately. It would make anybody very angry and maybe you hate your mother for that, possibly without realizing it.

Man

You mean, unconsciously, I'm guilty of disobeying the fifth commandment: "Honor thy father and mother..."

Girlfriend

I don't know, maybe the word "honor" has more than one meaning, like possibly "respond in kind." Haven't you ever heard the expression "Honor an insult with an insult?"

Man

That's interesting, I never thought of that. But I think that when the Bible was written down that the word "honor" had only one meaning. Also who knows what the Hebrew word for honor meant?

Girlfriend

Speaking of the Bible, are you aware that most people misinterpret the biblical "an eye for an eye"? Most people feel that it means at least an eye for an eye, while I have heard it said by some savants that it means at most, or no more than, an eye for an eye.

Man

You seem to know a lot about religion.

Girlfriend

No, but I like to go to church. It is a good place to meet men who are okay.

Man

To get back to my mother, are you saying that I have transferred the negative part of my feelings toward my mother onto all women?

Girlfriend

Yes, and also, possibly that your anger toward my date was a transference of your repressed anger toward your mother onto the therapist.

Man

But what about the mistakes he made?

Girlfriend

I accept the fact that your first therapist was not a good one, but does his being a lousy therapist justify your killing him.

Man

Boy, you're tough? Are you finished?

Girlfriend

No, as far as there being no women in your life there could be other reasons. The fact that your mother wouldn't call the doctor when you had an asthma attack indicates that there were probably other things in your childhood that were problematic and would bring about a personality development that would make interactions with the opposite sex harder than necessary.

Man

You seem to know a lot about psychology.

Girlfriend

I am a psychiatric nurse and, also, when you have psychological problems, you read up and learn about psychology.

Man

Okay to get back to my childhood, there were other things about my childhood which were problematic that could certainly be part of my problem with women.

Girlfriend

Can you give me an example?

Man

If I got hit by a kid and told my mother, she would say, "The next time you tell me a kid hit you, I'm going to hit you."

Girlfriend

Maybe she was trying to get you to fight back, although her reaction would certainly make it difficult for her to win the mother of the year award. How about giving me another example where her behavior was really unequivocally bad, besides your treatment when you had asthma attacks.

Man

Okay! Once I got my lip split open playing basketball. My mother did not think it necessary for me to go to a doctor to get stitches. When I would go to school, my teacher would ask me, why I had not gone to a doctor. This went on for several days. Finally, my mother told me to tell the teacher that I had an aunt who was a nurse who said I didn't need to go to a doctor. Of course, I didn't have an aunt who was a nurse, but I told the teacher that I did have one who said I didn't need to go to a doctor. Needless to say, I didn't get stitches and ended up developing a scar and had to stop playing the trumpet.

Girlfriend

That sounds bad. Maybe your parents were worse than the therapist.

Man

Now wait a minute, parents can't help what they are, but a therapist should be able to.

Girlfriend

Okay, but what about your job causing your women problems? Some men are too busy or too absorbed with their work to give finding a woman the effort it deserves.

Man

That might be a problem in my case.

Girlfriend

What do you do for a living?

Man

I do scientific research involving the application of mathematics to crystallography.

Girlfriend

My experience with research scientists at the hospital, we have some, since we are connected with a university, has taught me that research science is very demanding and some men, who do it, never find the wherewithal to go out and get a woman.

Man

Yes, I know. I always feel like a beginner, learning what I need to know to succeed as a researcher.

Girlfriend

You know, I just realized another reason why you had a problem with the therapist. He felt threatened by you because you are so bright; most men are going to feel inferior to you in the brains department.

Man

You mean because I am a mathematician.

Girlfriend

Yes, also your manner, despite your having killed my date tonight, is very genial, which would make many men, oddly enough, be jealous of you and therefore feel threatened by you.

Man

I have noticed that a lot of men seem hostile to me when we first meet and I have done nothing to them. I always wondered why. Now I think I understand.

Girlfriend

So where do we stand. Do you really feel justified in blaming your first therapist for your problems with women?

Man

The second therapist thought so.

Girlfriend

But he might be wrong. Another thing, you know that you give an overall impression of being innocent and defenseless. This would cause a lot of people, especially unhappy people who don't have a lot going for them, like your first therapist to abuse you.

Man

I know that.

Girlfriend

You know, if your first therapist was so bad, why didn't you just quit?

Man

It is not so easy for people like me who don't trust their feelings to just quit a therapy, and also, until I decided that he was bad, I felt that I should not give up and stick with it.

Girlfriend

Okay, but what about us, I can't believe I am saying this. Would you have approached me if you hadn't killed my date, your first therapist? Look what you did. You killed a man, followed me home and knocked on my door.

Man

I don't know. Did you notice me following you? It was quite a walk from the theater area to your apartment.

Girlfriend

Not really, I was too concerned about getting home.

Man

You know, if you had taken a cab, I might not have been able to follow you.

Girlfriend

I guess not.

Man

I'm glad you didn't take a cab.

Girlfriend

You know, if you are caught, you could go to jail for the rest of your life.

Man

But what about the fact that an impulse just came over me and it was not premeditated?

Girlfriend

How do you think the police, a judge, and a jury will feel about that?

Man

If you don't say anything about me to the police, I might never be caught.

Girlfriend

That could get me into trouble. Do you want to drag me down with you?

Man

No, I would never hurt you.

Girlfriend

All right, I have an idea.

Man

What's that?

Girlfriend

If we get married, then I couldn't be asked to testify against you.

Man

That's right. Let's get married.

Girlfriend

Do you want to spend the night with me?

Man

Yes. But what if I can't "ring your bell" or do anything for that matter; it's been a long time since I've been with a woman?

Girlfriend

Let's find out.

Man

Why don't we just get married first?

Girlfriend

Not to seem too forward, let us go to bed tonight and check out the marriage thing tomorrow.

Man

Really!

Girlfriend

Yes, Really! Now stop talking and let's go to bed.

(They walk out together.)

Scene 2

At Rise: Office with two detectives and a therapist.

First Detective

Okay Doctor, tell us why you are here.

Therapist

I read about the murder of that therapist downtown and I think I know who did it.

Second Detective

How do you know this? Were you a witness to the crime?

Therapist

No, but I think it was one of my old patients.

First Detective

Isn't any information that you can give us protected by doctor-patient privilege?

Therapist

I thought that since a homicide is involved and also, since the patient never said anything about the killing to me, that doctor-patient privilege did not apply. Furthermore, my association with the patient ended before the killing of the therapist.

First Detective

All right, tell us what you know.

Second Detective

Shouldn't we call the District Attorney's office and have an ADA here before the doctor starts talking?

First Detective

Let's see what the doctor has to say before calling an ADA. Go ahead, Doctor, talk to us.

Therapist

As I said, I had a patient who prior to my treating him went to the therapist who was killed.

First Detective

Don't many people go to several therapists; if one can't help them, then they go to another?

Therapist

Yes, that is certainly true.

Second Detective

So what's unusual about your patient and the therapist who was killed?

Therapist

The therapist who was killed made a terrible mistake with the patient and I helped the patient to realize how much hatred he had deep down for the murdered therapist because of the mistake.

First Detective

What was the mistake?

Therapist

The doctor allowed what is known as "countertransference" to occur in the therapy, which caused the patient immeasurable harm.

Second Detective

"Countertransference" what's that? I've heard of transference but never "countertransference."

First Detective

Transference, isn't that where the patient supposedly falls in love with the therapist?

Therapist

Not exactly! Transference is where the patient develops feelings toward the therapist, which (looking at first detective) you have characterized as falling in love, but they can be negative feelings like hatred, besides positive ones like love.

Second Detective

So what is "countertransference"?

Therapist

Well, transference is where feelings flow from the patient to the therapist; while "countertransference", on the other hand, is where feelings flow in the opposite direction, from therapist to patient. Also, in the case of therapists dealing with patients, transference by the patient of feelings onto the therapist is usually an integral part of a successful therapy, while "countertransference" usually causes problems.

First Detective

If "countertransference" usually causes problems in a therapy, why don't therapists avoid it?

Therapist

That seems to be almost impossible.

Second Detective

Why is that?

Therapist

A therapist is a living human being and therefore feelings flowing toward the patient are almost unavoidable; and these feelings give rise to "countertransference."

First Detective

Shouldn't the training of therapists include developing the ability to avoid "countertransference"?

Therapist

You would hope, but it doesn't seem to work that way.

First Detective

So if "countertransference" is so common, and I presume that patients' killing their therapists is not so common, why in this case did it lead to a killing?

Therapist

Usually therapists try to minimize the effects of "countertransference" or, hopefully the "countertransference" wasn't that bad; however, in this case, it was exceptionally bad and had a very deleterious effect on the patient.

Second Detective

What was the effect?

Therapist

The therapy made it impossible for the patient to ever develop a good relationship with a woman.

First Detective

"Countertransference" can do that.

Therapist

In my opinion, in this case, it did.

Second Detective

When you said in your opinion does that mean some therapists would disagree with you?

Therapist

Yes, especially the ones who are guilty of gross forms of "countertransference" with their own patients.

First Detective

I don't understand. You report on an ex-patient of yours who you think killed his previous therapist, and yet you also seem to defend the patient almost to the point of excusing the killing.

Therapist

I do have mixed feelings.

Second Detective

Can you explain why you have these mixed feelings?

Therapist

On the one hand, murder is a crime. On the other hand, the behavior of the murdered therapist toward the patient was unconscionable. The therapist indulged himself in such an egregious form of "countertransference" that once the patient realized what the therapist had done to him, it was almost understandable what happened.

First Detective

How long after the separation of the patient from his old therapist did the killing take place?

Therapist

Almost ten years.

Second Detective

Why so long?

Therapist

The patient didn't realize what the therapist had done to him for a long time

First Detective

Was the patient going to you as a therapist at this time when he did realize it?

Therapist

Yes.

Second Detective

You said before that you were instrumental in the patient's realizing what the previous therapist had done to him. Can you explain that?

Therapist

Yes, I went over the details of the therapy of the patient with the earlier therapist, and both the patient and I became aware of the malpractice of the previous therapist in dealing with him.

First Detective

Then you might be partly responsible for the patient killing his old therapist.

Therapist

In a way, yes, but I hope that I am not criminally responsible.

First Detective

No I don't think you are, but now we have to call for an ADA before we go on.

Second Detective

Okay, I'll make the call.

Scene 3

At Rise: Office with the same two policemen as in the previous scene and the girlfriend of the victim.

First Detective

You were on a date with the victim the night he was killed?

Girlfriend

Yes.

Second Detective

(Showing the woman a picture of a man.) So tell us, is this the man that killed your date?

Girlfriend

(After some nervous hesitation by the girlfriend.) No.

First Detective

Your body language tells us something different. People go to prison because body language gets them convicted of something.

Girlfriend

I'm nervous.

Second Detective

I feel that you are not telling us the truth. Do you know what perjury is?

Girlfriend

Yes I know what perjury is. But I promised him that I would not identify him if he didn't kill me.

First Detective

But that promise was made under duress, you are not obliged to keep that promise.

Girlfriend

But I swore on my life that I would not identify him.

First Detective

Let's talk about something else. Were you and the victim very close?

Girlfriend

Well, we were seeing each other, but I was beginning to feel that the relationship had to end.

Second Detective

Why is that?

Girlfriend

He wasn't a very nice man.

First Detective

In what way?

Girlfriend

He was very opinionated, wasn't very sympathetic for a doctor, and I don't think he was a very good therapist.

Second Detective

Why do you say that?

Girlfriend

I have had a lot of therapy myself, and I could sense that he had too many of his own problems that could and would easily spill over onto his patients.

First Detective

What happened the night he was killed?

Girlfriend

After leaving the theater that night, we walked toward his car.

Second Detective

The killing occurred a considerable distance from the theater district on an isolated street. What was the reason for that?

Girlfriend

Even though he was a doctor and made good money, he was cheap and didn't want to park his car in a lot where he would have to pay.

First Detective

So tell us what happened.

Girlfriend

This guy came up out of nowhere and had a pipe in his hand and before my date could do anything, he was hit on the head with the pipe.

Second Detective

Then what happened?

Girlfriend

The guy looked at me, raised the pipe to hit me, but I said, "Please don't kill me, I swear on my life that I'll never identify you."

First Detective

Then what happened.

Girlfriend

He just stared at me, and then he left.

Second Detective

Do you know what an accessory after the fact is?

Girlfriend

What do you mean?

First Detective

For being an accessory after the fact you could go to jail for 10 or more years. How old are you, thirty?

Girlfriend

I'm thirty-two.

Second Detective

You'd be about forty-two when you got out of jail. You're very good looking now, but you might not be so good looking when you got out of jail after ten years.

First Detective

Again, is this the man who killed your date? (Showing her the picture again.)

Girlfriend

All right! Yes he is.

First Detective

Thank you.

Girlfriend

Can I go now?

First Detective

No. We don't believe that he just left after he killed the doctor. There's more. Isn't there?

Girlfriend

Yes, there is more.

First Detective

Can you please tell us?

Girlfriend

He followed me home, and knocked on my door.

Second Detective

What happened then?

Girlfriend

I let him in.

First Detective

You let him into your apartment. Weren't you afraid?

Girlfriend

No, if he was going to kill me, I thought that he would have done it when he killed my date.

Second Detective

Then what happened?

Girlfriend

We talked?

First Detective

Is that all?

Girlfriend

No, he spent the night with me.

Second Detective

What did you say?

Girlfriend

We spent the night together.

First Detective

Did he force you?

Girlfriend

No, it was consensual.

Second Detective

How did that come about?

Girlfriend

He kept saying how beautiful I was, and I felt sorry for him.

First Detective

Are you also saying that you like him?

Girlfriend

Yes, I do like him.

Second Detective

How do you explain that at one point during the night when the murder occurred you were so frightened that you said to the murderer that if he doesn't kill you, then you would never identify him, and then a little while later you and he go to bed together without him forcing you?

Girlfriend

On taking a second look at him, I could tell that normally he was the kind of person that most people would consider harmless.

First Detective

But how could he be harmless and yet kill somebody?

Girlfriend

I guess everybody has their breaking point, even people we think of as harmless. I remember when I was a kid, there was this skinny kid with glasses that another kid, who was bigger, would pick on unmercifully; until one day The guy looked with glasses reached his limit and fought back. He did get the crap beat out of him, but he never got picked on again by the bigger kid

Second Detective

(Speaking to the first detective.) I think we have reached a point where we should have an ADA present.

Girlfriend

And I am beginning to think that I have said too much. I think I should get myself a lawyer before I say anything more.

First Detective

Yes, you should. Do you know someone you can call?

Girlfriend

Yes I do.

Second Detective

Good! There are phones in the hall, you can make your call from there and I'll call the DA's office for an ADA to come over.

(The Girlfriend and the Second Detective leave.)

(Curtain to end Act I)

Act II
Scene 1

At Rise: Courtroom

Opening statements of prosecutor and defense.

Prosecutor

The defendant murdered a therapist in cold blood by hitting him with a metal pipe. The defendant admits to the murder but the defense is claiming that there were mitigating circumstances and that the defendant acted under the impetus of a dissociative reaction, or in less technical terms, an "irresistible impulse." The reason given by the defense is that the defendant felt that the therapist had hurt him very badly in the therapy that the defendant had with the therapist. The state feels that there are not sufficient mitigating circumstances to justify such a brutal murder. If a patient thinks a doctor has made a mistake, then the patient has the right to bring a civil suit against the doctor. That's why doctors have malpractice insurance.

Defense

The defense feels that the therapist who was murdered made a gross miscarriage of therapy by making a very serious mistake. The mistake was in allowing what is called "countertransference" to intrude itself into the therapy. Before explaining what "countertransference" is, it is necessary to explain the term

"Transference." Transference is the phenomenon in therapy where a patient transfers emotions, sometimes inappropriate ones, onto the therapist. Therapy then, hopefully, helps the patient to resolve those emotions that are inappropriate and in doing so help the patient to solve some of his psychological problems. "Countertransference," on the other hand, is where the therapist has inappropriate emotions toward the patient and these can have very deleterious effects on the therapy, which they did in the case of the defendant. In the case of the defendant, the miscarriage was so great that the defendant was overpowered by an "irresistible impulse" when he saw the therapist at a theater and followed him to a place where the murder took place. Therefore the defense asserts that the defendant is not guilty by reason of temporary insanity.

Scene 2

At Rise: Courtroom

Prosecutor questioning therapist for the state.

Prosecutor

As a practicing therapist in this state for over 20 years, tell us what you think about what has occurred in this trial up to now.

Therapist for the State

Before his therapy, the defendant was the kind of person, who finds it almost impossible to express anger. He was a walking victim, because the inability to express anger makes him a "sitting duck" for all the people who want to take advantage of this weakness, and there are many. His therapist sensed this. Hence the therapist's job was to make him so angry that he finally could be brought to the point of expressing anger. This was the only option. When a person goes to talk therapy, there are three things he can get: a friendly ear, good advice, and the benefits of a process. The first two need no explanation. The third one, which I called the process, involves transference. Unfortunately, transference can create an agonizing situation which the defendant went through. Finally, the defendant reached the point where he expressed his anger at the therapist appropriately. It could be that his therapist precipitated a rather abrupt ending to the therapy, which did not give the patient time to integrate into his personality a new found capability to express anger when necessary. But, his therapist was not fully aware of what was happening. I do not think he can be blamed for this, since he acted in a very human way of dealing with an incident of the defendant's explosive anger, albeit long overdue as a result of years of repressing it. Finally, as far as the defendant's problems with women, I do not think it can be blamed on his difficulties with his therapist. The latter might have added to his difficulties with women but there seem to be possible other causes for it, like anger toward his mother. In fact it is also possible that the defendant's anger was primarily based on transference of his anger toward his mother onto the therapist. To go one step further, however, even to blame the mother may be unjustified. Parents are never perfect, and to blame them for all the things that can go wrong when bringing up children is ridiculous. Parents give children life and that's a lot, because most everybody no matter how difficult their life is would rather be alive than not. How many people in prison, if given a choice between life imprisonment without the possibility of parole or the death penalty, would choose the latter? The answer is that most would choose the former. Hence, it is my considered opinion that the defendant killed his therapist, not because of an "irresistible impulse" based on so-called "countertransference," but that he did it out of ordinary, yet still controllable, anger toward the therapist and is guilty of second degree murder.

Prosecutor

The prosecution rests.

Scene 3

At Rise: Courtroom

Defense questions therapist for the state.

Defense

I was struck in your previous testimony that people should be grateful for their parents giving them life. Is that all that one should expect from parents?

Therapist for the State

There are limits, of course. I am not justifying child abuse by parents.

Defense

All right, let's go on. A therapist for the defense will testify that the defendant killed his old therapist when acting under "irresistible impulse." You and he disagree about this. Why should the court believe you and not the other therapist?

Therapist for the State

Because most talk therapists would agree with me.

Defense

Have you ever had any therapies where "countertransference" was a problem?

Therapist for the State

I have had patients where there might have been "countertransference" but it never was a problem.

Defense

What about other therapists, do some of them ever have patients where there were problems with "countertransference"?

Therapist for the State

A few.

Defense

Any chance that the therapists who agree with you, about "irresistible impulse" not being the cause of the defendant killing his old therapist, had problems in therapies with "countertransference" and don't want to admit it?

Therapist for the State

No.

Defense

How can you be so sure?

Therapist for the State

I'm sure.

Defense

Is it possible that "countertransference" is the biggest problem in talk therapy?

Therapist for the State

No.

Defense

It's not even a possibility?

Therapist for the State

Maybe it's a small possibility. The biggest problem in talk therapy is how seriously disturbed a patient is.

Defense

Why is it that more and more therapist are avoiding talk therapy and doing other forms of therapy like drug therapy, especially if they are psychiatrists?

Therapist for the State

Because there seems to be no other way to help certain patients.

Defense

Don't they also make more money because they can treat two to four patients in an hour instead of one?

Therapist for the State

Yes, that's true.

Defense

Does drug therapy cure patients or rather just make them more comfortable?

Therapist for the State

Psychotherapy can't cure all psychological problems.

Defense

So with some patients, drug therapy is just a palliative and does not lead to cure.

Therapist for the State

You might say that.

Defense

We seem to have strayed a little from "countertransference." I assert that the most common reason for lack of cure for patients who go for talk therapy is "countertransference" and that was the problem with the defendant and his old therapist.

Therapist for the State

I disagree.

Defense

Can you prove that I am wrong?

Therapist for the State

No, I can't prove that, just like you can't prove that you're right.

Defense

We will have to let the jury decide that.

Therapist for the State

Yes.

Defense

I have no more questions for this witness.

Scene 4

At Rise: Courtroom

Defense is examining the therapist who
reported the defendant to the police.

Defense

Doctor, tell us what you think happened between the
defendant and his therapist.

Therapist

The defendant acted under, in psychological terms, a
dissociative reaction, or in less technical language, an
"irresistible impulse" when he killed his therapist and should
be judged not guilty by reason of temporary insanity?

Defense

Is the defendant insane?

Therapist

No, he committed the killing when he was only temporarily
insane as a result of being so mistreated by the therapist.

Defense

What could the previous therapist have done that was so bad
as to make the defendant act under an "irresistible impulse"
and kill him?

Therapist

The previous therapist indulged himself in what is known as "countertransference" with the defendant as you indicated in your opening. This went on for several years.

Defense

Can you give us a layman's explanation of the term "countertransference"?

Therapist

In layman's terms it means the therapist made a very bad mistake, caused by his own problems, which hurt the patient very much.

Defense

What was the upshot of this?

Therapist

After the therapy with the previous therapist, the defendant was never able to establish a good sexual relationship with a woman.

Defense

Are you saying that the cause of this problem with women was "countertransference" on the part of the previous therapist toward the defendant during his therapy?

Therapist

Yes.

Defense

Are you sure?

Therapist

Yes.

Defense

How can you be so sure?

Therapist

I spent a lot of time with the defendant and heard what his previous therapist did to him.

Defense

Can you describe what the previous therapist did to the defendant?

Therapist

In technical terms the old therapist exacerbated the Oedipus complex of the defendant by playing the role of a disapproving father making it impossible for the defendant to establish a satisfactory relationship with a mother surrogate, namely another woman.

Defense

Isn't the Oedipus complex derived from an ancient Greek play where a son kills his father and marries his mother?

Therapist

Yes, but in modern parlance, a son doesn't kill his father, just maybe resents him, and goes out and finds a suitable woman not his mother, but a substitute for her. In the defendants case it became impossible to get a suitable woman because of the mistake made by the therapist.

Defense

Can you explain in detail how this came about?

Therapist

An incident came up where a woman that the defendant liked seemed to give him a possible opening to make contact with her. The patient, as he described it to me, froze and didn't try to take advantage of the situation. Also, he didn't realize what he was doing at the time (by repressing what had happened). He reported the incident that day to the therapist who said nothing at the time. Then a few days later when the patient realized (or in technical terms stopped repressing) what had happened, he brought up the issue of what he had done and why he had not responded. This was a recurrent problem with him and he thought this would be a good example of his problem to use to try to change his behavior in these situations. The therapist refused to discuss it saying that nothing had happened. The patient, and I think rightfully so, then told the therapist that the therapist was saying the incident never occurred because the therapist (subconsciously) felt guilty about not immediately making the patient aware of what he had done and exploring the situation with the patient. This then, unbelievably, led to years of arguing about this one incident.

Defense

How is this "countertransference"?

Therapist

For one reason or another, the therapist could not admit that he had made a mistake and because of this, there was a feeling of anger of the therapist toward the patient. This then, in the curious way that the subconscious works, has the therapist become the disapproving father preventing the son from getting the woman of the incident who would be a substitute for the mother. This led to the patient having greater and greater problems with women which eventually led to women becoming off limits to him.

Defense

But don't a lot of men have problems with women, especially if the women appeal to them?

Therapist

Yes, but not as bad as the defendant's problem; and, if they do, then they sometimes go to a therapist for help.

Defense

And if they don't go to a therapist or get help some other way, what happens?

Therapist

They don't have good relationships with women, unless they are lucky somehow.

Defense

Does that mean, that once the defendant thought (in his subconscious) that the therapist had exacerbated his problems with women to the point where he felt that he probably could never get a woman, that when he, one day accidentally crossed paths with the therapist, killed him under the impetus of an "irresistible impulse"?

Therapist

Yes. And it didn't help that when the defendant crossed paths with the therapist the therapist was with a very beautiful woman, the kind of woman the defendant would have liked to get for himself. I guess he felt subconsciously that if he could not have a woman, why should his old therapist be able to have one, and such a beautiful one at that

Defense

Why do you think the defendant didn't kill the woman the therapist was with? Without her eyewitness identification, there would be no direct evidence against him.

Therapist

He is basically not a violent man and couldn't bring himself to kill her, even at the risk of getting caught; and, by the way, as far as I am concerned, this proves that when he killed the therapist he was acting under an "irresistible impulse."

Defense

(Looking at audience.) Some or all of you on the jury are wondering if the woman, who the therapist was with (his girlfriend) the night he was killed, will be called as a witness. This will not happen, since the defendant has admitted to killing the therapist and therefore she is not needed for these proceedings. Furthermore, as per the Judge's instructions, for reasons that cannot be revealed, nothing more will be said about the girlfriend by either myself or the prosecutor.

Therapist

I wondered why the girlfriend was not on the witness list for either the prosecution or the defense.

Defense

That is not for you to concern yourself with, Doctor.

Therapist

I think I understand.

Defense

I have no more questions for this witness.

Scene 5

At Rise: Courtroom

Prosecutor is questioning therapist who
reported the defendant to the police.

Prosecutor

Even though you were the one who reported the defendant
to the police, you seem to have a great sympathy for him. You
have said that you believe his killing his old therapist was the
result of an "irresistible impulse"?

Therapist

Yes I did.

Prosecutor

Then why did you essentially turn him in? He might never have
been caught if you hadn't reported him.

Therapist

I felt obliged to.

Prosecutor

And you don't feel you violated doctor-patient privilege?

Therapist

No.

Prosecutor

What exactly did the victim do that was so bad that it resulted in his being killed?

Therapist

He indulged himself in a particularly destructive form, as already indicated to the court, of what is called "countertransference" in therapy and it hurt the defendant very much.

Prosecutor

If this is true, then why was there such a long time between the end of the defendant's therapy with the first therapist and the defendant's killing him?

Therapist

He didn't realize how much his therapy had hurt him until he came to me as a patient.

Prosecutor

I once saw a television show, where a therapist brainwashes a patient into believing that her father had sexually molested her when she was a child, when in reality he hadn't?

Therapist

I saw that show. It was excellent with a great actress playing the therapist.

Prosecutor

Any chance you brainwashed the defendant into believing that his previous therapist had been bad, which resulted in his being killed, when he wasn't really that bad.

Therapist

In my opinion, no chance whatsoever.

Prosecutor

How can you be so sure?

Therapist

Because I have devoted the majority of my career to dealing with patients who have had unsuccessful talk therapies, like the therapy that the defendant had with the therapist he killed, and who come to me to repair the damage.

Prosecutor

Why do you do this?

Therapist

Because it is needed. Some people, who go to talk therapy therapists, come out of it not only not helped but hurt very much.

Prosecutor

Do you feel this way about most medical specialties?

Therapist

No. Most medical specialists are very effective. The practice of talk therapy or psychoanalysis is one of the exceptions.

Prosecutor

And why is this?

Therapist

Psychological problems are very difficult to treat; and, also many people who go into the practice of the kind of therapy that is called talk therapy sometimes have problems of their

---

own, which spill over into a patient's therapy, causing the ugly specter of "countertransference" to rear its ugly head as it did with the defendant.

Prosecutor

Don't therapists have to have a training therapy to avoid problems like this from happening?

Therapist

Not all therapists have a training therapy as part of their training; and even if they do, it might not help for various reasons.

Prosecutor

You have described "countertransference" when you were questioned by the defense attorney; and it is not necessary to repeat any of your responses. But tell us how a patient feels when he is being victimized by "countertransference."

Therapist

He feels that his time and money are being wasted by the therapist endlessly avoiding what the patient feels is important, and a lot of anger is generated which the patient is unable to express. In the case of the defendant, an incident occurred where he froze up with a woman he was interested in and, when he realized what he had done, he wanted to explore why. The therapist refused to explore the situation saying that nothing had happened. All this has already been indicated.

Prosecutor

Why would the therapist do this?

Therapist

Because of "countertransference", which manifested itself in that he couldn't admit that he had made a mistake, which led to the therapist becoming angry at the defendant.

Prosecutor

It doesn't sound like enough justification for the defendant killing the therapist

Therapist

It isn't, but the defendant felt that this incident characterized his problems with women and hoped that by exploring this situation with his therapist he would find out why he had problems with women and maybe get over them. He felt that the therapist failed him.

Prosecutor

Could it have been that the woman hadn't really given the defendant an opportunity to respond to her?

Therapist

Of course, but checking out the situation, instead of freezing up and not responding, would have resolved that. I mean most men when they see a woman who appeals to them are capable of wishful thinking and imagining the woman is showing interest in them when she really isn't. And if they approach her and she doesn't respond, they back off.

Prosecutor

All right, so the therapist didn't help, but why kill him? Just because a therapist is not effective, does that mean he deserves to die?

Therapist

I didn't say he deserved to die.

Prosecutor

But you are saying that the therapist who was killed was responsible for the defendant having problems responding successfully to a woman.

Therapist

Yes.

Prosecutor

Could a therapist have had that much effect on a patient?

Therapist

In my considered opinion, based on many years of experience, absolutely.

Prosecutor

And you feel that this justifies the anger the defendant felt toward the therapist.

Therapist

Yes, the therapist endlessly avoided trying to resolve the mistake the defendant thought he had made. Furthermore, the defendant's life was on hold, waiting to get help from the therapist. Do you know that while the defendant was going to the therapist, more than half of his take home pay went to pay for it? This went on for years.

Prosecutor

So what happened eventually?

Therapist

After a while the defendant would come home from therapy and start cursing and screaming in his apartment. He told me that he once went out with a woman that lived on his floor in his apartment building, and when he asked her if anybody on the floor could hear him cursing and screaming, she said, "Yes, you are known as the man that screams in the night." It was amazing that she went out with him.

Prosecutor

Why didn't the defendant curse and scream in the doctor's office?

Therapist

It is not so easy to do that in the therapist's office, especially if the therapist objects to it. For example, this therapist in warm weather would leave his office window open, instead of using the air conditioning, and say that people in nearby offices would complain if the defendant raised his voice. Furthermore, if the patient was the kind of person that could curse and scream easily in a therapist's office, he probably would be the kind of person that would not need therapy.

Prosecutor

If a patient thinks the therapist has made a mistake, why is it necessary for the patient to raise his voice?

Therapist

Because, not only do we communicate by what we say but also, and this is very important, by how we say it. If a person is angry and doesn't use an angry tone of voice, some people will not realize that they have made him angry.

Prosecutor

All right, go on.

Therapist

Finally by gradually building up to it, the defendant one day was finally able to bring himself to curse and scream at the therapist in his office with the same intensity he had been doing when by himself.

Prosecutor

What happened then?

Therapist

The therapist, on that day, said that if the defendant was going to curse and scream like that in the office, the therapy would have to end. The defendant had the good sense to say, at least as far as I am concerned, okay let the therapy end and picked, unilaterally, a time - a couple of weeks in the future - when it should happen. When the time to end came the therapist said, in a matter-of-fact way, that he had only been kidding. But the defendant followed through on ending the therapy, feeling that the therapy was going nowhere and also that it was not necessary to continue. I agree with this.

Prosecutor

So the defendant ended with that therapist and eventually came to you.

Therapist

Yes, and I made him realize what had been done to him as far as trying to establish a good relationship with a woman. The therapist had, because of the oedipal complications, intensified the defendant's hesitation and avoidance reactions to women. So one day when he spotted the therapist out with a woman, he was so overcome by an "irresistible impulse" that he followed the couple to the therapist's car which was in an isolated place and picked up a pipe, laying in the street, and hit the therapist, killing him.

Prosecutor

So in a sense you are partly responsible for the murder of the therapist.

Therapist

You could say that.

Prosecutor

And maybe that's why you reported the defendant to the police.

Therapist

You are probably right, but I still feel that the crime was based on an "irresistible impulse" and should not be considered murder.

Prosecutor

Even if what you say is correct and the malpractice of the therapist caused it to become impossible for the defendant to have a decent relationship with a woman, is that an excuse for killing him?

Therapist

No, but would you want to live without good relationships with women?

Prosecutor

They're important but not necessary.

Therapist

I think most men would disagree with you.

Prosecutor

Do you feel that the therapist did what he did out of malice and not just incompetence?

Therapist

Yes, the defendant asked, several times, for the old therapist to check out the problem between them with another therapist, and the old therapist never did.

Prosecutor

And this was wrong?

Therapist

Yes.

Prosecutor

Would every therapist agree that the old therapist should have checked out this situation with the defendant with another therapist?

Therapist

No, some therapists would just consider that the defendant was indulging in what is called "negative transference"; namely, transference of negative feelings resulting from an earlier troubled childhood relationship onto the therapist.

Prosecutor

Well, I don't want to let this be a battle between experts; I want the jury, using common sense, to decide. But I have trouble believing that the therapist could have such a strong effect on the defendant as to make it impossible for him to go out and get a woman. Why didn't the defendant just quit therapy?

Therapist

You don't realize the power of the connection that develops between a patient and the therapist when in a talk therapy relationship. If the therapist is good this might bring about a cure or improvement. But if the therapist is not good, this could result in what the patient went through. As far as quitting is concerned the patient is locked in. This is because of the strong emotions produced in therapy like an accumulation of unexpressed anger or one might say, an "anger debt," and the fact that the patient has invested so much time and money in the therapy. Freud called this situation, Analysis-Terminable-Interminable. Think of a bad therapy situation as a bad marriage. It sometimes is, for some people, as difficult to get out of a bad therapy as it is to get out of a bad marriage.

Prosecutor

But no matter how bad the situation is, does it excuse murder. Consider a situation where a surgeon makes a mistake which leaves a patient paralyzed, would the patient be justified in killing the surgeon, if he could.

Therapist

It doesn't excuse murder and the answer to your question is no.

Prosecutor

What's different?

Therapist

The surgeon might have made a momentary mistake that was not correctable, once it was made. The therapist who was killed had many opportunities to correct what he was doing wrong.

Prosecutor

That's your opinion, which I, and probably a lot of therapists, disagree with.

Therapist

Okay.

Prosecutor

Is it possible that the defendant's problem with women is based on something else, like possibly that he is gay? Is he gay?

Therapist

He might have a gay component like most people according to Masters and Johnson but he is not what one would call gay.

Prosecutor

Are you gay?

Therapist

No, are you?

Prosecutor

If you don't mind, I'll ask the questions. Let's go on. What about the fact that the defendant is a mathematician and I have heard it said that mathematicians are notorious for having problems with women? Supposedly, the greatest mathematician of all time, Isaac Newton, had lots of difficulties with women. In fact, isn't there a saying that "mathematics is a jealous mistress?"

Therapist

Not all mathematicians have problems with women. The almost as great mathematician as Newton, Gauss, wrote beautiful love letters to the woman who eventually became his wife.

Prosecutor

All right, what about the fact that the defendant was the kind of person who could not express anger in his therapy or in life in general, until he finally was forced to do so because he got so angry at the "countertransference" and without the "countertransference" this would never have happened?

Therapist

Even if that were true the "countertransference" still could have intensified the defendant's problems with women, and the ability to express anger could have been developed in another way. Furthermore, because of the abrupt ending of the therapy, which was precipitated by the therapist, the patient never really learned how to deal with and express anger appropriately; and this could have led to the defendants killing the therapist.

Prosecutor

But, appropriately or not, the defendant did learn how to express anger and isn't it considered a fact by most therapists that the inability to express anger at all can be a very serious problem, causing physical problems like migraine headaches and ulcers among others, and also things like automobile accidents. My experience has been that when an automobile accident is a result of alcohol, there was usually some repressed anger which brought about the drinking.

Therapist

But that still doesn't justify the old therapist's behavior.

Prosecutor

That's for the jury to decide. I have no more questions for this witness.

Scene 6

At Rise: Courtroom

Defense Attorney is questioning defendant.

Defense

Tell us about the night the incident with your old therapist occurred.

Defendant

I went to a play in a downtown theater one night and on leaving the theater after the performance had ended, I saw my old therapist with a woman. The woman was very beautiful. For some unfathomable reason, I started following them. We got to an isolated street where it was just them and me. They didn't seem to notice that I was following them. I seemed to go into a daze. I saw a metal pipe on the ground and I picked it up and got near to them. When I got very close the doctor turned around and noticed me, and without realizing what I was doing, I hit him with the pipe.

Defense

Then what happened.

Defendant

I left but stayed close enough so I could follow the woman home. When she got home, I knocked on her door.

Defense

Why did you do that?

Defendant

I don't know why; it just seemed to happen.

Defense

Okay, then what happened?

Defendant

She let me in.

Defense

And?

Defendant

We talked.

Defense

Anything else?

Defendant

We ended up going to bed together.

Defense

Did you force her?

Defendant

No, it was consensual.

Defense

Do you realize that if you also had killed her, you might have not been caught?

Defendant

Yes, but I killed the doctor on an uncontrollable or "irresistible impulse" and would never have killed the woman.

Defense

Why was there such a long time period between your ending your treatment with the doctor and your killing him?

Defendant

It took me a long time before I realized what he had done to me.

Defense

What made you realize what he had done to you?

Defendant

I went to a second therapist, who has already testified about this for the court, who made me realize what had happened to me in my previous therapy.

Defense

You mean that you were not angry at the first therapist till you went to the second therapist.

Defendant

Oh, I was angry all right, but it was sort of unfocused anger; I use to curse and scream by myself without really knowing why.

Defense

Where would you do this cursing and screaming?

Defendant

Mostly in my car when driving. Although sometimes in my apartment. I tried not to do the latter for fear that people could hear me and think I was crazy.

Defense

You mean you would spontaneously start cursing and screaming by yourself.

Defendant

Yes, in fact that's why, although after a long time, I started going to the second therapist.

Defense

And it was in the second therapy that you became fully cognizant of what had happened to you in your first therapy?

Defendant

Yes.

Defense

And you think that your realization of your first therapist's malpractice is what set you off when you saw him at the theater and led to your killing him.

Defendant

Yes.

Defense

Were you aware of what you were doing when you hit the therapist with the pipe?

Defendant

No. It was a purely impulsive act. I just went blank and hit him with the pipe. I am really sorry. If I had just not blanked out, I would not have done it. I can't believe I did such a terrible thing.

Defense

The defense rests.

Scene 7

At Rise: Courtroom

Prosecutor questioning defendant.

Prosecutor

So you want this court to believe that you are not criminally responsible for killing your old therapist?

Defendant

Yes, I just lost it.

Prosecutor

Would you have killed the therapist if you hadn't gone to the second therapist and through him learned of what your first therapist supposedly did to you?

Defendant

I don't know.

Prosecutor

Were his actions as a therapist, criminal?

Defendant

I think so.

Prosecutor

If a doctor makes a mistake that is called malpractice, should criminal charges be brought against him?

Defendant

I don't know. But just as a therapist is nowadays considered guilty of rape if he or she has sex with a patient; so likewise in the case of what is called countertransference by a therapist, the therapist should also be considered guilty of rape (although in this case, "emotional rape").

Prosecutor

If an officer in the military makes a mistake in a battle and it causes several men to die unnecessarily, is that criminal?

Defendant

Again I don't know. But during the Vietnam War, didn't officers get "fragged" if they made a mistake that caused enlisted men to die unnecessarily?

Prosecutor

Was Robert E. Lee doing something criminal when he ordered Pickett's charge on the third day at Gettysburg? Think of all the confederate soldiers that were killed, and if not killed, mutilated losing arms and legs in that charge.

Defendant

I read that the southern commander in the field there, James Longstreet, could not bring himself to give the order to charge, verbally, that he just nodded his head when asked if the charge should begin; and, also, that Pickett himself after the charge never spoke to Lee again.

Prosecutor

Do you think those confederates who survived Pickett's charge, but lost parts of their bodies and maybe could never get a woman because of it, hated Lee?

Defendant

Again and again I don't know.

Prosecutor

Lee was a great general because he pushed to the limit and Pickett's charge was the one time he went too far. If he had never gone too far that one time, it probably would have meant that he was not pushing to the limit like he did when he gambled and won mightily at Chancellorsville, and he would have been just another mediocre general.

Defendant

Is this a history lesson?

Prosecutor

Could it be that you were the only patient of your first therapist that he had "countertransference" problems with?

Defendant

Is that an excuse for his behavior?

Prosecutor

Possibly, and don't forget that Lee's soldiers were for the most part draftees, while you of your own free will chose to go to a therapist. By the way, why did you go?

Defendant

I had a problem with a woman.

Prosecutor

What was the problem?

Defendant

We were going together and had reached the point where we had to get married or break up and I couldn't do either.

Prosecutor

You mean you lacked the courage to do one or the other.

Defendant

All right, yes.

Prosecutor

Could it be that your difficulties with your therapist were appropriate punishment for your not having the courage to bring a relationship to some sort of closure on your own?

Defendant

That's sort of cynical.

Prosecutor

Tell the court again what your first therapist did to you that was so bad?

Defendant

He kept jerking me around endlessly when I would bring up some incident which I thought was important to explore, where I felt he had made a mistake. Exploring this incident might have been key to my having a successful therapy. I kept trying to corner him to face up to what he had done but he kept twisting and turning to avoid the issue and so we never could resolve it.

Prosecutor

You know the average person would have just given up and quit going to that therapist. I am not a therapist but I wonder if your problem was that you had been looking for and finally found a thing you felt was a mistake of your therapist's and then latched onto that like a bulldog and never let go.

Defendant

But it was a mistake.

Prosecutor

Is it easy for you to admit your mistakes?

Defendant

No, but I am not a therapist. And I told him he was making a mistake and should check it out with another therapist.

Prosecutor

How do you know he didn't?

Defendant

The second therapist said the first therapist would have told me if he had.

Prosecutor

Oh really, I don't believe that. Not many people can openly admit they made a mistake.

Defendant

Okay, you disagree with what the second therapist says.

Prosecutor

Not to rehash what has already been said, what was the final result of what the first therapist did to you?

Defendant

It seems he made it impossible for me ever to have a good relationship with a woman.

Prosecutor

Even if that were true, did he deserve to die for that?

Defendant

No, but I killed him because of "irresistible impulse", not because he deserved to die.

Prosecutor

Supposedly, you learned from your second therapist that the first therapist was responsible for your not being able to have relationships with women. Do you think that all therapists would agree with him?

Defendant

I don't know.

Prosecutor

Couldn't there be another reason why you don't have relationships with women?

Defendant

What other reason?

Prosecutor

That you could never commit to a relationship.

Defendant

Well, I do have problems with commitment.

Prosecutor

I'll bet. How many books do you have that you have never read but are hoping to read someday?

Defendant

What does that have to do with problems with commitment?

Prosecutor

You see a book that interests you and you buy it, bring it home and then put it on a shelf and never get around to reading it. Don't you see how that ties in with your commitment problems?

Defendant

Couldn't it be that I just like to collect books?

Prosecutor

I guess you are going to read all those books when you grow up.

Defendant

Sometimes you get a lot out of a book by just browsing in it.

Prosecutor

Let's talk about women. Have a lot of women thrown themselves at you?

Defendant

Some.

Prosecutor

I get the impression you didn't take advantage of many of these situations. Do you know why?

Defendant

They either weren't my type; or if they were my type, I couldn't bring myself to respond appropriately when I had an opportunity.

Prosecutor

Why didn't you respond appropriately?

Defendant

I don't know. I guess I blame that on my first therapist and the "countertransference."

Prosecutor

So you think not responding appropriately was not your fault?

Defendant

Yes.

Prosecutor

Have you not only not responded but ran away from some women, even some that you liked?

Defendant

Yes, unfortunately.

Prosecutor

How do you feel about that?

Defendant

Terrible.

Prosecutor

But it never was your fault, only your therapist's?

Defendant

All right maybe it was partly my fault. I wish I hadn't run away from some of them.

Prosecutor

How about the fact that being a mathematician is another reason you do not have relationships with women? When you were young, you focused on learning mathematics instead of chasing women like most young men do. We know about the mathematician Isaac Newton and his problems with women.

Defendant

I did spend some crucial years just studying and because of that developing some bad habits, which I rather not discuss, but I am certainly not in the class of Isaac Newton.

Prosecutor

Why did you study mathematics?

Defendant

Because I felt that mathematics explains the ultimate secrets of the universe.

Prosecutor

And you wanted the security of knowing the ultimate secrets of the universe.

Defendant

You might say that.

Prosecutor

But that wasn't enough for you, you wanted women also, even though it is possible that the real progress of science is usually paid for by the essential celibacy of mathematicians.

I am going to let you in on something that might surprise you. I majored in mathematics in college and when I was near graduation I had a choice: to go on to graduate school in mathematics with all its precise perfection, but with no women, or go on to law school, and the loose slipperiness of words, and enjoy the pleasures of women. As you can see I chose the latter.

Defendant

There are happily married mathematicians.

Prosecutor

Are you sure?

Defendant

Well I haven't taken a survey.

Prosecutor

What about courage? Could it be that mathematicians with their need to understand the ultimate secrets of the universe, and you especially, find it difficult to do things just because they feel like doing it, where courage is required, but always have to be absolutely sure before they do anything?

Defendant

Yes I don't trust my feelings and there were times in my life when I wish I had had more courage.

Prosecutor

But you killed somebody; that took courage, although a sick and socially unacceptable kind.

Defendant

That was not me acting normally, but me acting under "irresistible impulse."

Prosecutor

Oh really; let's get to the bottom of all this: do you feel that there was any justification for killing your first therapist?

Defendant

I don't say that it was justified; it was a momentary impulse. But for years the therapist just toyed with me, wasting my time and money, refusing to deal with an issue that I thought got to the heart of my problems. It went on and on until I got so mad that I started cursing and screaming when by myself.

Prosecutor

So what did you do then?

Defendant

The therapy ended after I finally blew my stack in the therapist's office, and after a long while, I started going to another therapist who made me realize what had gone wrong with the first therapy, namely what is called, as has already been indicated, "countertransference" on the part of the first therapist.

Prosecutor

Do you know that most people, and some doctors, even, have never heard of the word "countertransference"?

Defendant

Yes, I didn't know the word until I began reading up on therapy to find out what was going wrong with mine.

Prosecutor

Couldn't it be that what your first therapist did to you was just normal human interaction where if somebody is too much of a victim type, like I think you are, he gets victimized until he learns how not to be a victim anymore, if he ever does? Your first therapist did exactly what he was supposed to do. He kept pushing you around until you finally learned how to express the normal human emotion of fighting back. You probably got more out of therapy than most people. Your problems with women have little to do with supposed mistakes that were made by your old therapist. You killed him because you blamed him, and unjustly I might add, for your problems with women.

Defendant

That's not true.

Prosecutor

We'll have to see how the jury feels about that. I am finished with the defendant.

Scene 8

At Rise: Courtroom

Defense and prosecution summaries.

Defense

Killing somebody is never good. Even in war it puts a heavy burden on some soldiers. The public is not in agreement about the death penalty for criminals or euthanasia for terminally ill people in pain. Nevertheless the dissociative reaction, or "irresistible impulse," in this case, has been allowed in the court as a mitigating cause for killing someone in certain circumstances. The case before you is one of those circumstances. Even if the "countertransference" did yield a benefit to the defendant of bringing about the acquiring of the ability to express anger, there are other ways of developing this ability, but the "countertransference" resulted in the defendant not being able to have good relationships with women. Hence the price paid by the defendant of having to live without women was unnecessarily high and resulted in the "irresistible impulse" of killing his old therapist. Therefore, members of the jury, if you accept this premise in any way, there is reasonable doubt, and your verdict should be not guilty by reason of temporary insanity.

Prosecutor

It is true that "irresistible impulse" in certain cases has been used as an excuse for killing somebody. I do not think that it applies in this case. Doctors make mistakes all the time. Even if the therapist who was killed was responsible for the defendant's problems with women because of so-called "countertransference," that does not justify his being killed. If a doctor's mistake is egregious enough then a malpractice suit can be initiated. But did the therapist really make a mistake. The defendant is the kind of person that gets abused, because he invites it, probably unknowingly. Most people sense this and try not to abuse him, but some people cannot control themselves, because of their own needs. If they meet a person like the defendant they cannot resist abusing him. The therapist sensed this weakness in the defendant and forced him to express real anger for the first time in his life. Since most therapists agree that the ability to express anger is critical to overcome this weakness of letting people abuse one, the therapy worked. In other words the defendant was cured by what his old therapist did. Hence he, the defendant, had no justification to kill his old therapist and therefore "irresistible impulse" was not in play just ordinary, controllable anger, which the defendant did not control. Therefore you, the jury, should bring in a verdict of guilty of murder in the second degree.

REDEMPTION

A Play in Two Acts

by

Arthur Ziffer

Characters

Sarah Aubrey, a police detective

John Coyle, a police detective

William Willis, a private citizen

Louise Fallow, a mother and wife

Paul Fallow, husband of Louise Fallow

Ellen Montieth, a prosecutor

Richard Larson, a prosecutor

Alfred Keen, a public defender

The same actress can play Sarah, who only appears in the first act, and Ellen, who only appears in the second act.

Similarly, the same actors can play John and Paul, who only appear in the first act, and then play Richard and Alfred, who only appear in the second act.

The play takes place in the dead of winter on two successive days in a suburb of a northern city.

ACT I

At rise: Two detectives, John Coyle and Sarah Aubrey, are talking in a room in a police station. It is the middle of winter. The previous night was very cold. Sarah has just hung up the telephone.

Sarah

Well, they're all coming to the station.

John

Good. I can understand the Fallows coming here, being that it was their daughter, but I'd have thought that Willis would've resisted coming.

Sarah

He sounded like the kind of person who'd find it difficult to say no to the police. Maybe we should recommend that he bring a lawyer with him.

John

No, let's talk to him first, and if things get sticky we can stop the questioning and suggest his getting a lawyer.

Sarah

What did you think of the Fallow's reaction when we had them down to identify their daughter's body?

John

The mother seemed to take it much harder than the father.

Sarah

What a terrible thing, to have your daughter freeze to death so close to the city.

John

You wouldn't think things like that could happen.

Sarah

Well, it was very cold last night, and she wasn't dressed right.

John

But if she'd walked just a few miles south, she'd have come to Norwood, and she could've knocked on somebody's door.

Sarah

Maybe she didn't know which way to go.

John

But what about somebody stopping and giving her a ride?

Sarah

I guess people don't stop anymore. Maybe they're afraid.

John

I can understand not picking up a man, but a woman? What's to be afraid of?

Sarah

Some car-jackers purposely use a woman to get a car to stop, and then the car-jacker jumps out of hiding, or maybe the woman herself is the car-jacker.

John

Yeah, like what happened out in Fairburn the other night.

(The Fallows, Paul and Louise, enter the office.)

Sarah

Thank you both for coming down again. We hate to bother you at a time like this.

Paul

What more do you want from us? We've already identified our daughter.

John

There is one complication we need to resolve before we close the case.

Paul

What complication?

Sarah

The examination of your daughter's body, besides telling us that she froze to death, also revealed something that bothered us.

Paul

What was that?

John

Your daughter had a business card clutched in one of her hands.

Paul

A card?

John

Yes, it was a Yellow Cab business card.

Paul

So, our daughter was hoping to come across a phone and call for a cab.

John

Yes, that's what we thought, but the complication is that the card has a license plate number written on the back of it.

Paul

A license plate number? Do you know whose it was?

Sarah

Yes, we do. It was the license plate number for a car owned by a William Willis. Do either of you know him?

Paul

No.

John

How about you, Mrs. Fallow?

Louise

No, at least I don't recognize the name.

Sarah

We've asked him to come to the station. He should be here shortly.

John

Maybe one of you knows him by sight.

Sarah

The important thing is why your daughter had a card in her hand with his license plate number written on the back of it.

John

Furthermore, the writing was very sloppy. What was your daughter's handwriting like?

Louise

She had fairly neat handwriting.

Sarah

We think she wrote the number after she'd been in the cold for a while. Her writing indicated this.

Louise

Oh, my poor daughter. This is your fault, Paul. You shouldn't have fought with her before she went out yesterday.

Paul

Quiet, Louise.

Louise

You were always fighting with her.

Paul

Louise, shut up!

Louise

My daughter froze to death because you forced her to go out last night just to get away from you.

Paul

Well, who was she out with last night, and what happened to her date?

Louise

I don't know. Because of you, she never let us meet the guys she went out with. She'd meet them outside. She probably had a problem with some guy and jumped out of his car.

Paul

Am I to blame because she went out with some jerk that let her leave his car on such a bad night?

(William Willis walks into the office.)

John

Mr. Willis?

William

Yes

John

Thank you for coming to the station. I'm Detective John Coyle. This is my partner, Detective Sarah Aubrey. This is Mr. and Mrs. Fallow.

William

Why did you call me? It was very upsetting to get a call from the police.

Sarah

I understand. We called you to come to the station to ask you a few questions. We thought it would be less upsetting than if we came to your residence.

William

Questions? Questions about what?

John

Last night, a dead girl was found on Gramercy Lane. It seems that she froze to death.

William

That's terrible but what's that got to do with me?

Sarah

In one of the girl's hands was a Yellow Cab business card with your license plate number written on the back.

William

My license plate number.

John

Yes, do you have any idea why that is?

William

No.

Sarah

The girl's name was Imogene Fallow. She's the daughter of Mr. and Mrs. Fallow.

John

Did you know her?

William

No.

Sarah

Mr. Willis, do you know either of the Fallows?

William

No, I don't. I've never seen either of them before.

John

Have you ever seen Mr. Willis before?

Paul

No.

Sarah

What about you, Mrs. Fallow?

Louise

Not that I remember.

John

The big question is, why did the deceased have a card in her hand with your license plate number written on it?

Sarah

Mr. Willis?

William

I don't know.

John

Were you out last night, Mr. Willis?

William

Yes, I went to a movie.

Sarah

Were you with anybody?

William

No, I went alone.

John

What movie did you see?

William

The latest James Bond movie.

Sarah

What theater did you see this at?

William

At the Trinity Multiplex.

John

Did you see the early or late show?

William

The late show.

Sarah

Do you remember what time you got out of the theater?

William

It ended around eleven thirty.

John

Did you go right home?

William

No, I went for a bite at Al's Diner just down the road from the movie theaters.

Sarah

What did you do after you left the diner?

William

I went home.

John

Did you go home by way of Gramercy Lane?

William

Why do you ask?

Sarah

Do you have a problem answering that question, Mr. Willis?

William

Didn't you say the dead girl was found on Gramercy Lane?

John

Yes, we did. Did you, by any chance, on your way home, drive on Gramercy Lane and see anything? From your address, I can tell that one of the possible routes you could have taken to go from Al's Diner to your apartment would take you along Gramercy Lane.

William

Wait a minute. Before I answer any questions, should I get a lawyer?

Sarah

Mr. Willis, we just want to find out why your license plate number was written on the back of a card in the dead girl's hand.

John

Did you go home by way of Gramercy Lane?

William

I could have.

Sarah

Did you, or didn't you?

William

All right, I did.

John

Did you see a girl on the road?

William

Well, yes, I did see a girl trying to thumb a ride.

Sarah

Did you stop for her?

William

Well, no.

John

Why not? You saw a girl on a cold night trying to get a lift, and you didn't give her one?

William

No, I didn't.

Sarah

May we ask why not?

William

I usually don't like to pick up hitchhikers.

John

And why is that?

William

I just don't like to do it.

Sarah

Were you afraid to?

William

All right if you must know, yes.

Paul

You chicken-shit son-of-a-bitch. You let my daughter freeze to death because you were scared to give her a ride. What were you afraid of?

Sarah

Do you normally pick up hitchhikers, Mr. Fallow?

Louise

No, he doesn't.

Paul

But it's not because I'm afraid, at least not of a woman.

Sarah

What's your reason?

Paul

I just don't feel like giving people lifts; I might have to go out of my way.

John

Mr. Willis, do you have any idea why the deceased had your license plate number?

William

No.

Sarah

Did you slow down when you were driving by her?

William

Yes.

Sarah

Did you feel like stopping and giving her a lift?

William

Yes.

Paul

So, why didn't you?

William

I'm really sorry about your daughter. I wanted to stop and pick her up, but I just couldn't bring myself to do it.

Paul

Fuck you, you son of a bitch.

John

Take it easy, Mr. Fallow.

Sarah

Mr. Willis, were you afraid that the girl was just part of a car-jacking scheme?

William

No, my car isn't new enough to be a high car-jacking risk.

Sarah

So, what were you afraid of?

William

Uh! (Hesitating)

Sarah

Tell us, Mr. Willis.

William

I'm embarrassed to say.

John

Mr. Willis, a girl froze to death last night because no one stopped to give her a lift.

William

I, uh...

John

For God's sake, tell us.

William

All right, I'll tell you. I'm deathly afraid of letting a strange female get into a car with me when I'm alone.

Sarah

And why is that?

William

God, I'm so ashamed of myself.

Sarah

Come on now, Mr. Willis.

William

I know it sounds crazy, but I'm afraid I might be accused of rape.

Sarah

You mean when you haven't done anything?

William

Yes.

Sarah

Do you think many women would do this?

William

No, but some would.

Sarah

Do you feel anxious about the idea of being alone with a strange woman?

William

Yes.

Paul

You fucking nut case. A woman can't just accuse a man of rape. There'd have to be evidence of sexual contact.

Sarah

That's not true, Mr. Fallow. It's possible for a man to be convicted of rape when there's been no evidence of sexual contact, like transfer of semen.

John

Mr. Willis, would you give a male hitchhiker a lift?

William

More likely than a woman.

Paul

You fucking faggot.

Sarah

Please, Mr. Fallow.

John

You are aware, Mr. Willis, that most people would be more afraid of picking up a man than a woman.

William

I know. But the way I look at it is that the worst a man could do is rob me. But if a woman claimed that I raped her, what defense would I have? It would be her word against mine. I could end up in prison for a long time.

Paul

Do you have a girlfriend, Mr. Willis?

Sarah

We'll ask the questions, Mr. Fallow.

(Willis does not answer.)

John

Well do you, Mr. Willis?

Sarah

Considering your attitude about sex before marriage, I can't understand your asking that question.

John

It's different for men than for women.

Sarah

John, you're a hypocrite.

John

So you say. Mr. Willis do you have a girlfriend?

William

No, not right now.

Paul

Have you ever had one, asshole?

Sarah

I said we'll ask the questions, Mr. Fallow.

John

All right, Mr. Willis. I understand why you didn't give a lift to the girl, but do you have any idea why she wrote down your license plate number?

William

I think I know.

Sarah

Why?

William

When I drove by her, I stopped down the road in a rest area and waited to see if somebody else would give her a lift.

John

Why did you do that?

William

I felt guilty about not picking her up, and I wanted to see if somebody else would.

Sarah

Did any other cars come by?

William

Yes, several.

John

Did any stop for her?

William

No! And some of them were couples. With another woman in the car, the men in the cars were safe; the other woman would be a witness. I can't believe none of them stopped.

Sarah

Could the girl see you at the rest stop?

William

Yes.

John

How do you know that?

William

Well, she was looking right at me, and after some cars drove by her without stopping, she started walking toward me.

Sarah

What did you do?

William

As she got closer and closer to me, I felt more and more anxious. Finally, I couldn't stand it anymore, so I drove away and went home.

Paul

You cocksucker.

John

Easy now!

William

I guess that's why she wrote down my license plate number. I was her last hope, and she was angry with me for abandoning her. I'm so sorry.

Sarah

Why didn't you call 911 when you got home? The police would've gone and gotten her.

William

They would know who called even if I didn't give my name and come after me thinking I had done something to her.

John

Then why not call from a payphone somewhere outside your apartment? If you didn't give your name the police could never trace you.

William

Oh God. I didn't think of that.

Sarah

So you just went to bed and forgot about the situation.

William

No. I couldn't sleep. I stayed up all night, thinking about her, wondering if anyone picked her up. I even got in my car and started driving toward where she was, but I couldn't bring myself to go there. After a while, I turned around and went back home.

Louise

Oh, God, I'm being punished.

Paul

Shut up, Louise.

Louise

I've got to tell them. I can't bear it any longer.

Paul

Louise, I order you to shut up.

Louise

I can't go on like this. I have to tell.

Sarah

What do you mean, Mrs. Fallow?

Paul

Louise, you'll make trouble for us.

John

Quiet, Mr. Fallow, let's hear what your wife has to say.

Paul

Louise, don't tell them.

Sarah

Quiet, please. Is there something we should know about, Mrs. Fallow?

Louise

This is a sign. I need to let it out after all these years.

Paul

Louise! Don't.

Louise

I have to.

Sarah

Go ahead, Mrs. Fallow.

Louise

When I was a young girl, I let a man go to prison for supposedly raping me when he really hadn't.

John

Tell us about it, Mrs. Fallow.

Louise

I was nineteen and very much in love with someone. His name was Larry and he was twenty. He was in love with me, and he wanted me to sleep with him. I wanted to, but I wasn't like most of the other girls. I was still a virgin. And my father was very strict. Anyway, I finally agreed to do it when my parents were going to be away one weekend. But they came home early, and my father caught us in bed together. I was so scared that I said it was not consensual. I just blurted it out in a moment of panic. And, because my father was involved, I could never bring myself to tell the truth.

Sarah

That wasn't very bright to try to do it in your parents' home. Couldn't you have gone to a motel?

Louise

My boyfriend, Larry, and I didn't have a lot of money. Also, I would have been embarrassed to go to a motel.

Sarah

What happened to your boyfriend?

Louise

He would've gotten off without jail time if he'd just plead guilty. I begged him to do it, but he refused.

John

What sentence did he get?

Louise

Five to ten years.

Sarah

Considering both of your ages and the previous relationship between the two of you that sounds awfully harsh.

John

I don't think so. Just because a woman is willing doesn't mean it's not rape. Rape doesn't have to be forcible. I mean, look at statutory rape. When a woman lives in her father's house, she has no right to have sex. If she wants to do that kind of thing, let her move out. None of my daughters better have sex while they're living in my house.

Sarah

Sometimes I wonder about you, John.

John

I come from the old school, and I'm not ashamed of it.

Sarah

Good for you, John. Mrs. Fallow, it's hard for me to accept the fact that your boyfriend had a chance to escape jail time if he had pleaded guilty and then gets a sentence of five to ten years. Something seems wrong.

Louise

Well, there was a problem with the judge.

Sarah

What kind of problem?

Louise

It turned out that Larry once had a run-in with the judge.

Sarah

What do you mean by a run-in?

Louise

Larry accidentally bumped into a person one day at the central train station while he was walking and looking up at the departure board. And, before he could apologize, the person he'd bumped into started hitting him and Larry blew his stack and started hollering at the person. A policeman came up and separated them, and they went their separate ways. Larry swore to me that man he bumped into was the judge at his trial.

Sarah

Was this brought up at the trial? If that was true, the judge should have recused himself.

Louise

It was brought up at the trial, but the judge denied the run-in with Larry and said the defense was making the story up because they knew that he, the judge, was very tough and prided himself on stiff sentences.

Sarah

Did the defense try to get the policeman who separated them to give evidence? Policemen usually know all the judges, and usually a policeman who's stationed at a train station is there permanently.

Louise

Larry couldn't give enough information to track down the policeman.

John

Well, where is Larry now?

Louise

He died in prison.

John

Died?

Louise

He was raped in prison by someone who was HIV positive, got infected, and finally died of AIDS.

Sarah

Sounds like you kept in contact with him.

Louise

I used to visit him in prison. He told me about the rape and that he'd been infected.

Sarah

Did you ever think of trying to get him cleared by telling the truth?

Louise

I did, after he'd been in prison seven years, when I thought the statute of limitations would take effect and I couldn't be charged with perjury; but by then he had AIDS, and he said he'd rather die in prison than be a burden on his family.

Sarah

How did you feel about that?

Louise

I felt terrible. I wanted to get him released and bring him home with me so I could take care of him till he died, but Paul wouldn't let me.

Paul

It would have cost me a fortune. Why should I have to pay for him?

Louise

But he was Imogene's father.

Paul

So what? He never knew it, and neither did she.

Louise

Would you have said those nasty things to her last night if she had been your own flesh and blood?

Paul

She lived in my house. That meant she was supposed to do what I told her to do.

Louise

And now she's dead.

Paul

Shut-up, Louise.

Louise

Oh, God. I'm so sorry. And now I've being punished. God, forgive me. I've been a coward. I let my father frighten me into doing a terrible thing. A man I loved died in prison because of me. I thought of him every day. He never knew that Imogene was his daughter. I wanted to go to the authorities and get him released, but I couldn't bring myself to do it. Finally, he died in prison. And it was all because of me. Meanwhile, I went on with my life. I married a man who turned out to be - yes, Paul, you are - just like my father, and I let him try to dominate my daughter just like my father dominated me. Only my daughter had more guts than I did. She tried to fight back, and I didn't help her. Paul, I let you antagonize her to the point where she went out on such a terrible night. And now my little girl, my baby, is dead. She froze to death all by herself in the middle of the night. The only child I'm ever going to have is dead. Oh, God, (starting to cry) please forgive me, forgive me, forgive me.

Sarah

Don't be so hard on yourself, Mrs. Fallow; sometimes fathers can be very overbearing.

John

Sarah, I'm going to tell the lieutenant that this case is closed.

(John exits.)

Sarah

Mr. Fallow, would you come with me? We have to do some paperwork. Mrs. Fallow and Mr. Willis, just wait till Mr. Fallow and I return and I think you'll be able to leave.

(Paul and Sarah exit.)

William

I can't tell you how sorry I am about your daughter.

Louise

I know, but I'll never forgive you, Mr. Willis.

William

I understand.

Louise

Have you always been afraid of women, Mr. Willis?

William

I've been afraid of being alone with a woman for almost ten years.

Louise

Not your whole life. Can you remember why it started?

William

Yes.

Louise

Can you tell me? I think you owe me that.

William

I owe you that and a lot more.

Louise

So what was it?

William

I was very attracted to this woman, but I hadn't pursued her very effectively. She finally got so fed up with my clumsy approaches that once when I called her up, probably at a very inappropriate time, she yelled at me. Then, crazy as it sounds, I found myself driving over to where she lived. I think I was going over there to propose to her. But when I got there she had gone out, and her father answered the door, and when he found out that I was the one his daughter had yelled at, hollered at me and told me that I should stop bothering his daughter. I left and went home. But then I began to feel a most excruciating anxiety that she'd come over to my place and accuse me of rape.

Louise

Did she come over?

William

I don't think so, probably not.

Louise

You don't know?

William

No.

Louise

How come?

William

I felt so much anxiety that I had to leave my apartment and stay at a motel. From then on I seem to have the phobia.

Louise

And because of that my daughter is dead.

William

I'm so sorry.

Louise

I hate you.

William

I don't blame you.

Louise

But do I have the right to hate you?

William

What do you mean?

Louise

I couldn't stand up to my father and save a man from going to prison.

William

But you were dealing with a real fear that of what your father would do to you, while I was running from a sick, imaginary one.

Louise

Oh, I don't know. What would my father have done to me? Beat me or force me out of the house? I doubt it.

William

Wait a minute. Listen to how Detective Coyle talks about his daughters.

Louise

I heard him, but tell me, what is the worst possible thing that could happen to you if your so-called sick, imaginary fear came to pass?

William

That I would go to prison for the rest of my life.

Louise

That's something to be afraid of. That's a lot worse than my father beating me or forcing me out of the house.

William

You know there are cultures where if a woman loses her virginity while living in her father's house, she runs the risk of being killed by her father and or her brothers.

Louise

I know that. But I was afraid of admitting to perjury, which would have just resulted in a few years in prison, not a life sentence like you were worried about.

William

Thank you for being easy on me, but I'll never forgive myself for leaving my apartment and going to a motel that night.

I feel I should've been able to fight the fear and stay in my apartment that night.

Louise

Isn't there an old saying: if you're afraid of something then it will very likely happen?

William

That's frightening!

Louise

Not to indulge in, what might be called psychobabble, did it ever occur to you that maybe you were so angry with the woman for rejecting you that a part of you wanted to rape her, and what you were running from was the fear of that part of yourself?

William

One of the many therapists that I've been to once suggested that possibility.

Louise

Do you agree?

William

I didn't then, but I do now.

Louise

Did therapy help you?

William

No my therapeutic experiences were disasters.

Louise

How so?

William

Do you know what countertransference is?

Louise

I think so; it's where the problems of the therapist spill over into the therapy.

William

Yes that's it, that's a very good way of describing it.

Louise

Do you know that in a play of Israel Horovitz, there is a line where it is pointed out that the word therapist is made up of two words: "the" and "rapist"?

William

That's interesting. But I am tired of blaming therapists for not curing my problems. I'm sure that's just an excuse for not doing the things that are necessary to resolve one's problems.

Louise

What things are you referring to?

William

Well, in lieu of good therapy, which seems hard to come by, it seems to me that the only way to resolve your own psychological flaws is to take a look at yourself while you're having anxiety.

Louise

You mean examining yourself when doing things that have an element of danger.

William

Yes.

Louise

Have you done things like that?

William

Yes, but it always seemed that I didn't do enough of them, and I always held back when it might have done some good.

Louise

What kind of things are we talking about?

William

Things like rock-climbing, spelunking, scuba diving, and parachute jumping.

Louise

What's spelunking?

William

Cave exploring in non-commercial caves.

Louise

Those things sound scary to me and I don't think they are necessary to get over one's psychological problems

(Paul enters.)

Paul

Louise, you're wanted in the room 208 to finish up the paperwork.

(Louise exits.)

Paul

I really hate your guts.

William

I understand your anger, Mr. Fallow, and I'm really sorry about the death of your daughter. I mean, Mrs. Fallow's daughter.

Paul

Imogene had my name, and she was born after her mother and I were married. That made her my daughter, at least legally.

William

I don't think children should be thought of as possessions.

Paul

Oh fuck you. You know, if I saw a woman freezing to death, trying to get a lift, I'd have picked her up, fucked her, or at least tried to, and then taken her to where she wanted to go.

William

How can you talk like that when we're talking about your daughter, even if she wasn't your biological daughter?

Paul

You don't think much of me, do you?

William

You're not one of my favorite people.

Paul

You know, I knew a guy in Vietnam who you remind me of. I was his company commander. Like your fear of being alone with a woman who might accuse you of rape, he had a pathological fear of stepping on a land mine and getting his legs blown off.

William

I wouldn't call that pathological. I'd think that's a very normal fear.

Paul

But this guy was too much. Every time he was ordered to walk point, he'd turn white. In fact, after a while his sergeant stopped asking him to walk point. So I ordered the sergeant to order the guy to take point every time we moved. I loved to see that scared look on his face when he got the order.

William

That seems unnecessarily cruel. Why did you do that?

Paul

I thought it would toughen him up.

William

I would have thought the Army would not condone that.

Paul

They didn't. The jerk finally stepped on a mine, and the sergeant ratted on me. I thought that sergeant was tough. But he had a problem: he thought of all of the men as if they were his sons. The soft son-of-a-bitch.

William

So what did the Army do to you?

Paul

They gave me a dishonorable discharge.

William

I'd have thought that you'd have been sent to the stockade.

Paul

You know, you've got prison on the brain.

(Louise enters.)

William

What a piece of work you are, Mr. Fallow.

Paul

Hey, go fuck yourself. I didn't let a girl freeze to death because I was scared shitless to give her a lift.

Louise

Damn you, Paul, you're not so perfect. What about that little boy who fell off the Cape Storm ferry and drowned? You could've saved him.

Paul

Why should it have been me? What about his parents?

Louise

You were closest to him.

Paul

His parents should've been watching him more closely.

Louise

So they made a mistake. You still should have gone into the water to get the kid. You're a good swimmer, and his parents didn't look very athletic. I was really sorry then that I'd never learned how to swim.

Paul

Stop criticizing me. It was rough water, and who knows where the propellers are on a ferry.

Louise

I can still remember the look on that boy's face before he went under. There was such terror in his eyes. I'll never forget it. You must have seen it, too. I can't believe you don't feel guilty about that. Maybe that's why you've being so hard on Mr. Willis.

Paul

Take that two-bit psychology crap and shove it up your ass.

William

I don't think you should talk to your wife like that, Mr. Fallow.

Paul

Why not? Are you going to try and stop me, chicken-shit? Don't you think everybody knows why you're so afraid of going to prison?

William

What do you mean? What am I afraid of?

Paul

You're afraid that in prison you'd be a patsy.

William

What do you mean by a patsy?

Paul

You know what I mean. (Paul shapes his mouth like he's going to kiss someone and makes a kissing sound as he looks at William.)

Louise

That's cruel, Paul.

Paul

Oh, shut up, Louise.

Louise

Oh, you shut up!

Paul

Don't you tell me to shut up. (Paul slaps Louise.)

William

Hey, don't you hit her!

Paul

Don't you tell me how to treat my wife? (Paul slaps Louise again.)

(William steps in between Paul and Louise.)

William

Stop hitting her!

Paul

You're asking for it. (Paul hits William.)

William

How dare you hit me, you foul-mouthed son-of-a-bitch? (William hits Paul, and they begin to struggle.)

Louise

Stop it!

(Paul and William keep fighting.)

Paul

I'm gonna kill you!

Louise

Oh, God, somebody stop this!

(Paul and William get more and more violent until finally Paul falls down, hitting his head, and then lies still.)

William

(Examining Paul.) Oh, my God, I think he's dead.

(Detectives John Coyle and Sarah Aubrey come rushing into the room.)

Sarah

What's happened here?

(John examines Paul.)

John

Mr. Fallow is dead.

(Curtain to end Act I.)

Act II

At rise: Louise and William are alone in a room in the District Attorney's office complex the following afternoon.

William

I'm sorry about your husband. But he kept hitting me. All I tried to do was stop him.

Louise

It seemed like you did more than that. You were punching back.

William

What was I supposed to do? He just wouldn't stop.

Louise

So what did the police do?

William

Well, they put me in a cell for the night, and today they're going to arraign me.

Louise

What charge?

William

That'll be decided by the District Attorney's office. Two prosecutors questioned me all morning and are in another office deciding that.

Louise

Will you have a lawyer present?

William

Somebody from the Public Defender's office is coming.

Louise

Shouldn't you get somebody other than a public defender? Larry, my old boyfriend who died in prison, had someone from the Public Defender's office, and he seemed very inexperienced.

William

I don't know what to do. I don't know any lawyers.

Louise

So you spent the night in a cell?

William

Yes.

Louise

Were you alone?

William

Yes, thank God, but the damn cell was cold.

Louise

I know about cold jail cells.

William

Oh?

Louise

That's what did in my boyfriend, Larry, who I got sent to prison for no good reason.

William

What do you mean a cold jail cell did him in?

Louise

Well, Larry wasn't what you'd call a combative type, so when he first went to prison, he felt that he'd be safer if he were in solitary. So he requested it, and they gave it to him. He then started on a program of building himself up, spending all day in his cell doing push-ups. He hoped he could become so strong that he'd be able to stand up to any aggression. He got to be quite good at doing the push-ups, even getting to the point where he could do 125 of them at a time. The problem came when they moved solitary to a section of the prison that wasn't heated. The first winter in that kind of cell resulted in his being sick for months with some sort of bronchitis, so he requested to be put in the general population where they had heated cells. The prison authorities granted his request since he wasn't in solitary for cause. One day, he got caught alone by some prisoners who preyed on guys like Larry, and, despite all of the push-ups, he couldn't prevent himself from being raped. The rapists were HIV positive and infected with AIDS, and you know he eventually died from it.

William

Oh, my God! I hope I don't go to prison. Aren't you going to tell them that your husband started the fight and I was just defending myself?

Louise

I could, but some people would say you've killed my whole family, my daughter the night before last and my husband yesterday.

William

But I didn't do anything to your daughter.

Louise

You could have picked her up and driven her home.

William

I know. I'm so sorry about that. But I wasn't the only one who drove by her and didn't stop. Why am I more responsible for her death than any of the other people that drove by?

Louise

You knew she was in trouble. You stopped.

William

But there were other people who could've stopped and driven her home without taking any risk. I told you several couples drove by and didn't stop. Why didn't one of them stop? If it's a couple, the man couldn't be accused falsely with another woman there.

Louise

You really do have a phobia.

William

You know, I have to tell you this. There was something I didn't tell the police.

Louise

What?

William

There was a couple that drove by your daughter and slowed down as if they were going to stop.

Louise

And?

William

But the woman started acting very annoyed and pointed very forcefully for the man to drive on.

Louise

What happened?

William

The man seemed to resist a little, then he gave in and drove right by your daughter.

Louise

Oh, my God!

William

I was so annoyed at the couple that I wrote down their license number. Would you like me to give it to you? I have it here in my wallet.

Louise

You mean as witnesses of some sort?

William

No, for you to go and ask them why they didn't pick up your daughter, and also to tell them what that resulted in.

Louise

You know that very few women would let their husbands stop to pick up a strange woman.

William

I know, but I thought that the women's movement might have changed that.

Louise

You don't understand women.

(Prosecutors Ellen Montieth and Richard Larson and a public defender, Alfred Keen, walk into the room.)

Ellen

Well, Mr. Willis, you've caused quite a stir here. Mr. Larson and I seem to have a major disagreement over what you should be charged with.

Alfred

Hello, Mr. Willis. My name is Alfred Keen, and I am here from the Public Defender's office. I'm very sorry to be late getting here. There was a mix-up at our office, and before we knew it the morning had gone by. Ms. Montieth and Mr. Larson shouldn't have questioned you before I got here.

Richard

We were just trying to get some preliminary information.

Alfred

I'd like to confer with Mr. Willis alone.

Ellen

All right, Mr. Larson, Mrs. Fallow, and I will leave the room for a while.

(Louise, Ellen, and Richard exit.)

Alfred

Mr. Willis, you look like you can afford a more expensive lawyer than a public defender.

William

Your right but I like the way you talk, can I start with you and if things look like they're not going right, then you recommend someone, or would that be a mistake?

Alfred

Well, ok, let me see what the situation is and then, if necessary, I'll let you know if I think you should get somebody high-priced. Now, I've read the police reports, which were pretty complete. Sarah Aubrey, the woman detective who interviewed you with Detective John Coyle yesterday afternoon, wrote up a report that was favorable to you. Detective Coyle's report, on the other hand, seemed biased against you. But then, knowing the two of them as I do, that was to be expected.

William

I sort of felt that I'd get more sympathy from Detective Aubrey.

Alfred

What transpired when the detectives left you and the Fallows alone?

William

Well, Mrs. Fallow had to leave the room, and I had a conversation with Mr. Fallow when we were alone.

Alfred

And what was the conversation about?

William

It had to do with Mr. Fallow's experiences in Vietnam as a company commander. It seems he gave orders for somebody, I reminded him of, to walk point at every possible opportunity. The man eventually stepped on a land mine and Mr. Fallow received a dishonorable discharge.

Alfred

When did the fight start?

William

After Louise returned and before the detectives came back in, Mr. Fallow started being abusive to Louise, I mean Mrs. Fallow, and I tried to stop him. Then he started hitting me, and I fought back. I guess I fought back too hard.

Alfred

I think you should have known better than to get into the middle of a domestic argument.

William

But he was hitting her.

Alfred

Well, it's too late to worry about that now. The big question is what will Mrs. Fallow say? He was her husband, although Detective Aubrey's report seemed to indicate a deep rift existed between them.

William

Yes. It seems Mr. Fallow wasn't the father of the girl who froze to death and, according to what Mrs. Fallow said, he was less than ideal as a stepfather. I guess the report explained all that.

Alfred

Do you think Mrs. Fallow will describe the fight between you and Mr. Fallow as simply you trying to defend yourself?

William

I was hoping so, but when I spoke to her alone she seemed to feel that I fought back a little too much for just self-defense.

Alfred

They left you alone with Mrs. Fallow?

William

Yes, for a short time. It seemed almost by accident.

Alfred

That sounds odd to me. I wonder if they weren't observing the both of you.

William

Wouldn't that be illegal?

Alfred

I think so. It could be construed as entrapment.

William

Does everything depend on Mrs. Fallow?

Alfred

Well, if what she says is prejudicial to you, we could say that she's biased. Of course, if the rift between her and her husband was very deep, then maybe she will speak favorably for you. Stranger things have happened. I think we should hear what she has to say.

William

Ok.

Alfred

Is there anything else you want to tell me before I call them back?

William

I don't think so.

Alfred

Think isn't good enough. You have to be surer than that.

William

Ok, I'm sure there's nothing more to tell you.

(Alfred goes to the door of the room and speaks.)

Alfred

Ok, we're ready to continue.

(Louise, Ellen, and Richard walk back into the room. Richard, Ellen, and Alfred stand apart from William and Louise.)

Richard

I'll tell you right out, Mr. Public Defender. I'm leaning toward a second-degree murder indictment. I know about the soldier in Vietnam that Mr. Fallow use to make walk point at every opportunity who finally stepped on a land mine, and I think Mr. Willis identified with him. This led to such anger in Mr. Willis that he wanted to kill Mr. Fallow.

Ellen

No, that's crazy. In my mind, it's justifiable homicide or, at most, involuntary manslaughter.

Alfred

It's obviously a case of justifiable homicide.

Ellen

I'd like to hear what Mrs. Fallow says since she was the only witness to the fight.

Alfred

Is it likely that the wife of a man who gets killed in a fight is going to be an impartial witness?

Richard

Who knows, but let's hear what she has to say.

(Richard, Ellen, and Alfred move toward William and Louise.)

Ellen

Mrs. Fallow, what happened between your husband and Mr. Willis?

Louise

Paul, my husband, started being abusive to me, including hitting me. Mr. Willis tried to stop him, and then Paul started hitting Mr. Willis. Mr. Willis started fighting back. At one point, Mr. Willis hit Paul very hard and Paul fell down and hit his head.

Richard

Your husband just started being abusive to you out of the blue.

Louise

Well, he was cursing at Mr. Willis, and I guess I got fed up with it and said that he wasn't so perfect, and then I reminded him of something he'd done, which I feel was similar to Mr. Willis not picking up my daughter. This got him mad, and he started yelling at me and hitting me.

Ellen

What was the something you reminded him of?

Louise

We were on a ferry when a little boy fell in the water, and he didn't jump in to save the boy.

Richard

You think that's the same as not giving a girl who's freezing to death on the road a ride?

Alfred

That's her opinion. She's entitled to it.

Richard

I'm beginning to think that there's some sort of conspiracy here, that Mrs. Fallow and Mr. Willis joined together to get Mrs. Fallow out of a less than satisfactory marriage.

Ellen

But they never knew each other before they met yesterday afternoon.

Richard

A conspiracy doesn't have to be prearranged. It could just be the unspoken agreement between people who have equal minds about something.

Ellen

Richard, you're always bringing up these conspiratorial plots that aren't prearranged. Conspiracy implies prearrangement.

Alfred

Oh, is this a recurrent concern of Mr. Larson?

Ellen

Yes.

Richard

You know, Mrs. Fallow, you've admitted to having committed perjury concerning your boyfriend who went to prison and died there.

Ellen

But that was more than seven years ago, and the statute of limitations applies.

Richard

I don't know about that. Since the perjury resulted in a death, it could be that the statute of limitations doesn't apply. I'm going to talk this over with the District Attorney. Sometimes he and I see eye to eye on things.

Ellen

Richard, sometimes I wonder about your interpretation of the law. Mrs. Fallow isn't responsible for her boyfriend's death in prison.

Richard

Look, Ellen. The reason the District Attorney puts us two together is that we balance each other out. Don't try to make my conservative approach to the law as pathological. Your liberalism is just as offensive to me. Why aren't you working for the Public Defender instead of the District Attorney? That's where you belong.

Ellen

The District Attorney is interested in justice, not convictions.

Richard

We aren't sure what justice is in this situation. Mrs. Fallow, are you sure that you've told us exactly what happened? My feeling is that you're glad Mr. Willis got rid of your husband for you and are expressing your gratitude by saying that your husband was the aggressor.

Louise

Well, my husband was hitting Mr. Willis. What was he supposed to do?

Richard

I don't know. If I were responsible for the death of somebody's daughter, I'd probably let him beat the shit out of me, out of guilt.

Ellen

In the first place, she wasn't his biological daughter; and, secondly, I've never seen you to be anything but combative, even when you're obviously in the wrong.

Richard

So you say. (Looking at Louise.) Mrs. Fallow, how would you like to spend the next twenty years in prison for perjury?

Alfred

Hey, you can't threaten her like that.

Richard

Quiet! Let me finish. Do you want to change your story a little? Didn't Mr. Willis look for a chance to fight with your husband? Could it be that the story about the soldier in Vietnam who was made to walk point until he got his legs blown off was so upsetting to Mr. Willis that he lost it? I think Mr. Willis is a wimp and a loser. He saw an opportunity to get back at the kind of people who've been pushing him around his whole life, and he lost control. I'm going to do everything in my power to see that he gets a long sentence. Now, do you want to help me, or do you want to join him in prison for the next twenty years? And you won't be in the same cell with him.

Alfred

This is unconscionable.

Ellen

I agree, but would somebody explain to me exactly what walking point means?

Richard

It means that when a group of advancing soldiers move into possible enemy territory, they move in a straight line formation, one man leading and the rest spreading out behind him forming a straight line. The first man is said to be walking point and is usually the first to come across any land mines planted by the enemy.

Ellen

Okay, I understand.

Richard

Enough of military tactics. Mrs. Fallow, you're still relatively young and very attractive. You can find another man and still be happy in life. You don't want to spend your remaining sexually active years in prison, do you?

Ellen

Richard, stop that or I'll report you to the DA. I can't believe that he'd condone such tactics.

Richard

Tell me, Mrs. Fallow. Was your marriage a happy one?

Louise

Why do you ask?

Richard

You married a man when you were pregnant. Did you love him, or were you just desperate to get married?

Louise

I was scared. My father wanted me to have an abortion, but I didn't want to.

Richard

So was the marriage a happy one?

Louise

We had our problems.

Richard

Problems you call them. Tell me, did you love your husband as much as the boyfriend, Larry, you caused to go to prison, who was the father of your daughter?

Ellen

Hey, you shouldn't be asking questions like that.

Richard

Shut up. I know about you: you frigid bitch? That cop in the eighth precinct you used to go out with told me all about you.

Ellen

He was angry because I dumped him.

Richard

Does that mean he lied? (Looking at Louise.) Well, what about it, Mrs. Fallow, did you love your husband as much as you loved your boyfriend, or maybe I should ask if you loved your husband at all?

Louise

It's none of your business.

Richard

Are you afraid to answer the question?

Louise

All right, if you must know, I loved Larry and didn't love my husband.

Richard

Now I see it. You wanted to get rid of your husband, and Mr. Willis did you a favor. And now you want to show your gratitude by saying he killed your husband in self-defense.

Louise

It was self-defense.

Richard

Come on, Mrs. Fallow. Think back to that time when you were in love with Larry. Then you were married to a man for twenty years whom you never loved. But you knew what love could be like with the right man. I think you've been thinking about that all your married life.

Louise

There are other things in life besides love.

Richard

Oh really! Tell me what?

Louise

My daughter growing up and being happy in her own life.

Richard

But your husband fought with her the night before last, and she foolishly went out with the wrong guy who maybe made her get out of the car when she would not put out, and she ended up freezing to death. Now there's no daughter to live vicariously through and experience the joys of life at least through her life. You blamed your husband for that, so you provoked a fight between him and Mr. Willis, hoping for what did happen. I'm sure you've heard the saying, people want what is best for their children, but they want even something better for themselves.

Louise

That's not true, that's not true. I didn't provoke the fight. It just happened.

Alfred

I'm going to report this to the DA. You have no right to badger her like this. Ms. Montieth hasn't Mr. Larson gone off the deep end.

Ellen

I would certainly agree with that.

Richard

Look, you two goddamn queers, let me do my job.

William

What you're doing, Mr. Larson, is criminal.

Richard

(To William) Oh, yeah, I've seen the way you and Mrs. Fallow look at each other. Don't think I don't know what's going on. I have the feeling that if you both get off, then you'll get together. Well, I'm going to make sure that doesn't happen. Mr. Willis, I'm going to make sure that you get convicted of second degree murder. Furthermore, I think that in prison a man like you'll get raped, again and again, and get AIDS. Then, when you get real sick from it, they'll put you in a prison hospital bed and you'll just lie there in your own piss and shit and scream for medications that prisons can't afford and you'll die in agony like you deserve.

Ellen

That's a horrible thing to say.

Richard

Mr. Willis, did you ever see the older version of the movie "The Postman Always Knocks Twice"? If you remember, John Garfield is executed at the end for killing Lana Turner, who actually died by accident. And as he's walking to the electric chair, he realizes that he's being executed for the crime he got away with - killing her husband. Well, Mr. Willis, I'm going to make sure that you go to prison, not for killing Mr. Fallow, but because you didn't give a ride to his daughter.

William

What about the other people who drove by her and didn't pick her up? Are they guilty, too? Are they going to be punished?

Richard

Oh, my God, I don't believe you're saying this. You don't see any difference in what you did and what they did.

William

What about the couple that slowed down and then the woman made the man speed up and leave Mrs. Fallow's daughter to freeze to death?

Richard

I can't believe I'm hearing this. You think there's something wrong with a woman not wanting to let her husband give another woman a ride? You don't understand women. You belong in prison where there are no women.

Alfred

You know, Mr. Larson, you'd have been happy during the Spanish Inquisition. You might have even become the grand inquisitor.

Richard

That's just liberal ACLU crap.

Ellen

While you were talking, Richard, I couldn't help but wonder about your love life. Have you ever been in love?

Richard

What do you think?

Ellen

I don't think so. I can't imagine that anyone who has experienced the joy of life, like having been in a real loving relationship, would sound as vicious and bitter as you do.

Richard

I've been in love.

Alfred

Ever with a man?

Richard

How would you like to have your client sent to a maximum-security prison?

Alfred

For a prosecutor, you are pretty thin-skinned.

Richard

You know you all think Mr. Fallow was cruel to that soldier, making him walk point until he stepped on a land mine.

Alfred

The Army thought so. That's why he got a dishonorable discharge.

Richard

No, he got a dishonorable discharge because the Army found out about it officially.

Alfred

What do you mean?

Richard

Do you know about the old Army policy of "Don't ask, don't tell"?

Alfred

I think so.

Richard

What do you think it meant?

Alfred

It referred to the Army policy of forcing people to keep secret if they were gay or be forced out of the service.

Richard

Bingo! And do you know why the Army wanted to change that policy?

Alfred

Because maybe gay people can perform in the Army as well as straight people can.

Richard

Maybe, but have you ever wondered why so many men are willing to go and fight in wartime? Do you think they do it because of patriotism? That's crap. There's only one reason why a man will risk mutilation and dying in agony in war.

Alfred

And what's that?

Richard

You should know, you faggot.

Alfred

Why don't you just tell me?

Richard

Because they don't want to be like you. They hate the idea of always being afraid, and they go to war to fight it, to overcome whatever is in them that they think is making them that way. Why do you think Mr. Fallow made that soldier walk point all the time? Because he knew what the man's problem was and was giving him a chance to conquer it.

Alfred

Mrs. Fallow, did your husband ever talk about that soldier?

Louise

No, but we did go to visit him once in an Army hospital. He seemed to be unable to learn to use prosthetic legs and never left the veterans' hospitals.

Alfred

Why do you think he never learned to use prosthetic legs?

Louise

I think it was because the mine blew off his genitals, too.

Alfred

Was your husband upset about the man?

Louise

I think so.

Alfred

You think?

Louise

Well, we never went to visit him again.

Richard

Oh, shit! Did any of you ever see the movie "Johnny Got His Gun"?

Alfred

About the soldier who gets his arms and legs blown off, is blinded, deafened, and loses his jaw by a shell exploding near him?

Richard

Yeah, that's it. Look how much better off the soldier who stepped on the mine was than the guy in that movie.

Ellen

Richard, you're really gruesome.

Richard

Mr. Willis, which would have been harder for you to do: walk point in combat or pick up that girl? Which scares you more: stepping on a land mine or going to prison for rape when you didn't do it? I guarantee if you'd been in the Vietnam War and had to walk point, you'd have picked up that girl and given her a lift.

Ellen

How do you know he wasn't in the Army and maybe fought in Vietnam?

Richard

I guarantee that he wasn't.

Ellen

Mr. Willis?

William

No, I never was in the military.

Richard

See, I told you so.

Alfred

What about you, Mr. Larson?

Richard

I knew you'd ask that, you asshole!

Alfred

Well, are you going to answer?

Richard

Not only was I in the war, but I also volunteered for the Marine Corps, volunteered to go to Vietnam, and also volunteered every chance I got to walk point.

Alfred

Did it cure you?

Richard

You're fucking-aye it did.

Ellen

I guess that means yes.

Richard

Let's cut out the chitchat, and get down to business. Mrs. Fallow, are you going to change your story? Think about it. Think what spending the next twenty years in prison for conspiracy that caused the death of your husband. Although we both know that you'd really be going to prison because you perjured yourself and let your boyfriend go to prison and die. Do you like to have a drink now and then? A martini perhaps? There'll be none of that. Do you smoke? Soon they're not going to allow smoking in prisons. You're still a good-looking woman, but in twenty years you'll be an old hag. No man will look at you twice. Come on, let's put Mr. Willis in prison where he belongs. I'll tell you what. (Looking at William.) I'll compromise. Instead of second-degree murder, twenty-five to life, I'll go for voluntary manslaughter one, fifteen years. Mr. Willis, you'll get out when you're still in your fifties. Come on, you've been in prison your whole life anyway. No women. Afraid of this; afraid of that. Worrying about everything. Always thinking, never doing. Come on. Surrender. People like you belong in prison. Stop fighting it.

Louise

Mr. Larson, you seem to have an obsession with prison. You talk about years in prison so matter-of-factly. I think, deep down, you want to be in prison; I think you want to be in prison to prove yourself. You want to feel that you can take it like the men you sent to prison have to, that you could handle years being locked up. You know, deep down, that you want to be tested like that. Can't you volunteer to go to prison and put yourself to the test? Or, if that's not possible, then attempt to commit some crime. Bungle it so that you get caught, making sure, of course, that nobody gets hurt, but that you still get a long sentence. I'm sure that, as a prosecutor, you know what crime to attempt so you could end up in prison. You know you want this to happen so you can prove yourself. Come on. Surrender. People like you belong in prison. Stop fighting it.

Richard

Mrs. Fallow, I'm going to do everything in my power to make sure you get the longest possible prison sentence.

Louise

Why is it that I knew you'd say something like that?

Alfred

Mr. Larson, you're deranged. I'm sure when I go to the DA and tell him some of the things that you've been saying, you'll be charged with prosecutorial malfeasance. Of course, I'll need you, Ellen, to go with me to back me up.

Ellen

I will. Every so often, I think I should be working at the Public Defender's office. But then I know I have to stay with the DA so I can stop people like you, Richard, from abusing their power.

Richard

Say what you want now, but remember who you're up against. I volunteered to walk point in Vietnam, where the slightest mistake or bit of bad luck would've resulted in at least one or both of my legs being blown off. I lived with fear until I didn't feel it anymore. Would any of you have done that? I doubt it. But do as you will. Object to me all you want. Accuse me of prosecutorial malfeasance. But be ready for the consequences, for I guarantee, there will be consequences.

Alfred

Mrs. Fallow, are you still with us?

Louise

Yes, I am. Mr. Larson, I've let two controlling men make my life a shambles—first my father and then my husband. But it will never happen again. I'm going to fight you no matter what the consequences are. Mr. Willis, even though he's responsible in some way for the death of all my family, especially my daughter, which I'll never forgive him for, tried to protect me and then defend himself. I can't believe the law doesn't allow people to defend themselves. You, Mr. Larson, are crazy and are a disgrace as a prosecutor and I am going to expose you.

(Curtain)

ISAAC and AMANDA

A Play in Ten Scenes

by

Arthur Ziffer

and

Herbert Hauptman

Some of the material in this play is
taken from the already published play

"On the Shoulders of Giants"

by

Arthur Ziffer

and

Herbert Hauptman

CAST OF CHARACTERS

Catherine Barton, a niece of Isaac Newton

Clarissa Challoner, wife of the master counterfeiter Challoner

Robert Hooke, of Hooke's Law in Elasticity

Leibniz, German Mathematician and Philosopher

Isaac Newton

Amanda Taggert, a young, attractive, wealthy widow

SETTING: All the scenes take place in the living room of Isaac Newton's home in London.

Scene I

AT RISE: Newton is talking to the audience.

NEWTON

My name is Isaac Newton. I know some of you, upon hearing my name, will want to get up and leave, thinking that I am going to bore you with talk of mathematics and physics. Such is not the case. I am going to tell you about that period of my life when I decided to give up on the private life of being a scholar at Cambridge and entered into the public life of a government official in London. There were two reasons that this came about. Firstly, it was as a reward for my work in science, culminating as it did in the publication of the Principia. The Principia, for those of you who do not know, contains my Laws of Motion, which explain the motions of the planets. The second reason, or maybe this should be the first, was that the "powers that be" thought that I could be of some help in solving some of the problems that were plaguing English currency.

It did me no harm, of course, to be an associate of Charles Montagu, also known as Lord Halifax, in obtaining my position; although I certainly felt that I deserved it. The position was that of being Warden of the Mint, which was the second in command to the Master of the Mint, which I became several years later. The position of Warden was mostly concerned with the prosecution of counterfeiters and other criminals who were trying to profit through various illegal operations involving English currency.

Actually, what I am going to talk about is my relationships with women. Most people think, and I wonder why so many people are interested in this more than my scientific work, that I have had no relationships with women in the conventional sense. In Cambridge, it was easy to avoid women. However, here in London it proved to be more difficult. I guess a man is a fool to think he can get through life unscathed by women. And let's face it; most men would not want to. I certainly am glad that my lovely niece, Catherine, came to live with me after her mother, my half-sister, died. She is the light of my life. I even forgive her for the private conversation she had with one Amanda Taggert, a young, wealthy, attractive widow that John Locke, yes the famous philosopher and not so famous ladies' man, tried to arrange for me to meet.

Scene 2

AT RISE: Catherine Barton and Amanda Taggert
are having a very private conversation.

CATHERINE

Madame Taggert, you should not have come here. My uncle
got very angry with John Locke for trying to introduce you to
him. He was so furious that he wrote a letter to Locke, saying
that he wished that he, Locke, was dead, although he later
apologized.

AMANDA TAGGERT

Please call me Amanda. I am not that much older than you.

CATHERINE

As you wish, Amanda, but still you should not have come here.
What if my uncle should come home from the Mint early and
find you here?

AMANDA

I have come here to get your help.

CATHERINE

To get my help to do what?

AMANDA

To arrange a private meeting for me with your uncle.

CATHERINE

That I cannot do; he would never forgive me.

AMANDA

Wouldn't you say it is unusual that your uncle should feel such anger toward John Locke for trying to introduce him to a woman that he wishes Locke to die for it? Is your uncle usually so violent and extreme in his reactions?

CATHERINE

No, usually he is quite moderate, unless it involves science, mathematics, religion, or women.

AMANDA

I can understand the first three, but why women?

CATHERINE

I don't know; it seems that he avoids women.

AMANDA

But what about you; you live here, and he doesn't avoid you.

CATHERINE

That's different; I am his niece, and he is comfortable around me.

AMANDA

All right, but let me ask you if you do not feel smothered by your uncle? Don't you feel that he resents any man who pays attention to you?

CATHERINE

He is just trying to protect me.

AMANDA

Or is he trying to hold on to you?

CATHERINE

No, he wishes me to be happy.

AMANDA

Then, and I hope you do not find this question tasteless so soon after his untimely death. Why did you not marry Lord Halifax?

CATHERINE

I do not find the question tasteless; I have recovered from the shock of his demise.

AMANDA

Good, I suspected so since I hear that you are now engaged to be married to someone else.

CATHERINE

Yes! The answer to your question, however, is that Charles never asked me to marry him.

AMANDA

Was it because he did not love you?

CATHERINE

No, I'm sure that he loved me.

AMANDA

Then why didn't he ask you to marry him?

CATHERINE

I don't know.

AMANDA

Could it not have been because he knew the effect it would have had on your uncle if you married and you left to live with him?

CATHERINE

Possibly. It is true that my uncle, once he accepted the fact that I was going to marry John Conduitt, readily agreed to have John move in here after we are married.

AMANDA

Will that suit you?

CATHERINE

I would prefer that we lived apart from my uncle.

AMANDA

Not to change the subject abruptly, but did your uncle know that you were sleeping with Lord Halifax?

CATHERINE

Madame, you are embarrassing me. Please do not talk like that; I'm afraid of it getting back to my uncle.

AMANDA

Catherine, your secrets are safe with me. Besides, your uncle is the only person who doesn't realize how intimate your relationship with Halifax was.

CATHERINE

Amanda, please do not pursue this.

AMANDA

All right, but Catherine; it is time for me to tell you one of my secrets.

CATHERINE

What secret?

AMANDA

I have been in love with your uncle since I was a little girl.

CATHERINE

You knew my uncle then.

AMANDA

Yes, and it is not that long ago. Remember, I am not that much older than you.

CATHERINE

How did you know my uncle?

AMANDA

My father owned the tobacco shop in Cambridge where your uncle used to buy his pipe tobacco. I used to spend time in the shop to be with my father and I would see your uncle when he came there.

CATHERINE

And you knew him then.

AMANDA

In a way.

CATHERINE

What way?

AMANDA

He never spoke to me. When I was little, he would look at me and smile. As I grew up he would look at me less and less, sometimes only stealing a glance, until finally when I was fully grown he wouldn't look at me at all.

CATHERINE

So then you never spoke to him.

AMANDA

No but when he would speak to my father, I would strain to hear every word that he said. The sound of his voice was so entrancing to me.

CATHERINE

So what happened?

AMANDA

Because of your uncle, I made my father allow me to get an education. And I didn't only study the usual subjects that women study, literature and music; I studied mathematics and science in the hopes that I would meet your uncle and be able to talk to him about things of interest to him. But we never met. I tried to go to some of his lectures but women were not allowed to attend.

CATHERINE

But you married someone else! How did that come about?

AMANDA

Your uncle would never notice me. Once I saw him walking on the street and coming toward me. I stopped and smiled at him to give him an opportunity to talk to me, but he just averted his eyes, stared at the ground, and walked right by me.

CATHERINE

My uncle seems not to be interested in women.

AMANDA

Then why not be oblivious to me. I could accept that; but to cast his eyes down meant that he knew who I was and felt some attraction toward me, but for some reason was not going to do anything about it.

CATHERINE

And what happened after that?

AMANDA

So when some rich widower from London, visiting Cambridge to see his son, saw me and pursued me, I married him, thinking I would forget your uncle once I was married to someone else.

CATHERINE

Did you?

AMANDA

I did to some extent. But then when my husband died and I found out that your uncle was going to be in London at the Mint, all my old feelings for him returned. Please help me to have a private meeting with him.

CATHERINE

My uncle could become very angry with me.

AMANDA

You are on the verge of getting married. You can afford to risk your uncle's anger to free yourself. Do you want to let your fear of your uncle's ire ruin this relationship as, I do believe, you let it spoil the one with Halifax?

CATHERINE

Madame, are you going to talk to my uncle like you have just spoken to me?

AMANDA

I know you are afraid of him, but don't you think it is time some woman spoke to him like this.

CATHERINE

I don't know; I can't answer that question.

AMANDA

Please, Catherine, arrange a meeting between me and your uncle, for my sake, and possibly his, also.

CATHERINE

I hope that I do not live to regret this, but come next Sunday night. The servants are off and out of the house; I will arrange to be out also and leave the door unlocked. But I hope that you know what you are doing. My uncle sometimes has very strong reactions.

AMANDA

Trust me; I am sure that this will work out to everyone's advantage.

Scene 3

AT RISE: Newton is talking to the audience.

NEWTON

You are all probably wondering how I really feel about women. Now you realize I don't have a lot to talk about in this area, but there are certain things I feel the urge to talk about to try to understand myself better.

Before I went to Cambridge, there was a girl with whom I was friendly. Since it has been such a long time, I will mention her name, although I am embarrassed to say I do not remember her first name, a Miss Storer. I remember that she seemed willing to do anything that I wanted her to do. I did nothing; I was afraid that she would get pregnant and that I would then have to marry her and that would be the end of my going to Cambridge, although I did like her very much and have always had some regret that such a thing did not come to pass.

There were, of course since I was young, some women at Cambridge that caught my fancy. My mentor, Isaac Barrow (no, not all mathematicians have the first name Isaac,) had one of his nieces visit him one summer. I think he wanted to match me up with her. She was very attractive. I even think she liked me. I would meet her at his house every Sunday for afternoon Tea. Then we would go out for a walk. I could never think of anything to say. She would prattle on, and I would just enjoy the sound of her voice. Also, I was very intrigued by the sprightly way she had of walking. This went on all summer. It was just before the Plague years, when I was working out the Laws of Motion. The time came for her to return to her family. I was feeling very uncertain. I was on the verge of a great breakthrough, which turned out to be the case, but I had hit a snag in the work and was agonizing over it. It was the last Sunday before her return to her family. I came late to Tea. She tried to get me to look into her eyes. For some reason, I avoided looking into them; I don't know why. Then I sensed her getting angry. She finally left without saying goodbye, and I never saw her again.

No, that wasn't the only incident at Cambridge. There were others. There was this town girl in Cambridge whom I liked to look at. I would see her on the Commons on Sundays sometimes. I thought that eventually when I had the opportunity I would go up to her and introduce myself. One day, I saw her with another man. She looked at me nervously when he put his arm through hers. I knew most probably it was no more than a casual act, but for some reason which I cannot explain, I avoided the Commons from then on. I could go on and on, but I realize these stories would not be interesting to most people since essentially nothing ever happened. Also, I must admit that I got off easy in Cambridge. Such was not to be the case in London. The women in London were much more aggressive than in Cambridge. In my position as Warden of the Mint, I came up against a very determined woman who did not let me off so easily. As I have said, the job of Warden of the Mint was to deal with the prosecution of criminals involved in currency crimes and counterfeiting in general. The most notorious of these counterfeiters was a man named William Challoner. After much work and pressuring of witnesses, I managed to get enough evidence against this man that was sufficient to have him hanged. However, this no-good, hard-drinking, whoremaster had a wife who, difficult as it is to believe, came to plead for his life. I can remember how forceful she was. Luckily, my niece Catherine was present during the interview.

Scene 4

AT RISE: Newton is meeting with the wife of Challoner.
Catherine Barton is also present.

CHALLONER'S WIFE

I have come to plead for my husband's life.

NEWTON

I am sorry, but he deserves to die.

CHALLONER'S WIFE

But why? He has not killed anybody. Why should he have to die?

NEWTON

It is one of the possible punishments for his crimes.

CHALLONER'S WIFE

You could have just as well sent him to prison, and he would eventually be free.

NEWTON

How can you come here and plead for your husband? He is a profligate, and is forever committing adultery. Aren't you angry with him?

CHALLONER'S WIFE

Yes, I am angry at the way he goes with every willing woman that comes his way, and there seem to be so many that are willing. There is something about that smile of his. But I don't want to see him hanged. He is all that I have, and he always comes back to me after his little flings. Please, Sir Isaac, let him live, even if he goes to prison.

NEWTON

No, he has been sentenced to die.

CHALLONER'S WIFE

Sir Isaac, you have everything in life. You are not only the most famous scientist in England, I am told, but in the world. You are wealthy as well. And you are hale and hearty, still in your middle years. Why would you bother yourself with being Master of the Mint, wasting your time and energy on such mundane matters as counterfeiting when you could still be doing your great scientific work?

NEWTON

Madame, for the wife of a criminal, you are very well spoken. May I ask how does this come to be?

CHALLONER'S WIFE

My father is a minister and he made sure that I grew up with a reasonable education.

NEWTON

Then how did you come to marry a man like Challoner?

CHALLONER'S WIFE

I was like all the other willing women. All he had to do was give me that smile of his and I was captivated.

NEWTON

But does being captivated translate into marrying him and going from the comfortable middle-class position of a minister's daughter to that of being the wife of a ne'er-do-well, philandering, counterfeiter.

CHALLONER'S WIFE

There was also the problem I was having with my father at the time. He wanted me to marry some dull farmer who was very rich, but who never learned how to smile.

NEWTON

Do you regret having married Challoner?

CHALLONER'S WIFE

Sometimes, but it is too late for me to regret it; I am married to him.

CATHERINE

Uncle, what would be wrong in showing leniency to Challoner?

NEWTON

Well, for one thing, I would be besieged by petitioners for every counterfeiter that was to be hanged.

CATHERINE

Uncle, certainly that cannot be the reason.

NEWTON

All right, since you press me. The truth of the matter is that this man Challoner has made a fool out of us at the Mint for years with his clever tricks, and he does not deserve any leniency.

CHALLONER'S WIFE

Please, Sir Isaac, I beg you.

NEWTON

No, stop this!

CHALLONER'S WIFE

Please, Sir Isaac.

NEWTON

No, madam, no; I won't; I can't.

CHALLONER'S WIFE

Is there any chance that the severity of the punishment for my husband is because in some way you are envious of him?

NEWTON

Why would I be envious of a common criminal?

CHALLONER'S WIFE

Is it possible that having been a great scientist has not been enough for you, that you resent the fact that my husband has lived a life so very different from yours?

NEWTON

What specifically are you getting at?

CHALLONER'S WIFE

Could it be that you begrudge him the endless succession of women that he has had in his life?

CATHERINE

Madame, you are saying the wrong thing to my uncle.

CHALLONER'S WIFE

Am I? I hear that the great Sir Isaac is afraid of women. Why could he not see me without you being here?

CATHERINE

I warn you to watch what you say to my uncle.

CHALLONER'S WIFE

Not only will I not watch what I say, but I will go further. Sir Isaac, if you promise to release my husband I will do anything for you. Yes, I say this even with your niece present. Are you shocked? What would be the harm in it? My husband would not care and, even if he did, it would be my small revenge for all the times he played me false with other women.

NEWTON

I am not interested in anything that you could do for me.

CHALLONER'S WIFE

I do not believe that; I see the way you look at me; you are staring at me. I have not been married so long that I have forgotten what that look means. Do not be hesitant and shy, Sir Isaac. There is more to life than books and your scientific theories. All your great discoveries will only benefit the world. Live for yourself, Sir Isaac.

NEWTON

I do live for myself, madam; it is just in a different way than the way most people live. I am finding this conversation very unpleasant and I wish it to end.

CHALLONER'S WIFE

Sir Isaac, why are there no women in your life?

NEWTON

That is none of your business, you outspoken slut.

CHALLONER'S WIFE

Is there a good reason why there are no women in your life? These stories about you and that Frenchman, Fatio. Are they true? Is that what the great Isaac Newton is all about?

CATHERINE

Madam, how can you be so vicious.

CHALLONER'S WIFE

Sir Isaac, you coward, stop avoiding looking into my eyes. Being a great scientist does not relieve you of the obligation of being a man.

CATHERINE

Madam, this behavior is unconscionable.

CHALLONER'S WIFE

Don't try to squelch me you spoiled brat. Would you not do the same for your husband if you were married? Could you say that you love a man and not be willing to do this to save his life?

CATHERINE

I would never marry a criminal.

CHALLONER'S WIFE

Suppose he was not a criminal, would you do it then? Sir Isaac, I hear that you are a very profound student of Scripture, as well as a great scientist. Tell your niece that no less a person than the biblical Sarah, the patriarch Abraham's wife, slept with other men to save Abraham's life and, more, that she did it under the bidding of Abraham.

CATHERINE

That cannot be true and even if it was, it is sacrilegious for you to identify your husband with the patriarch Abraham.

CHALLONER'S WIFE

How dare you talk to me of sacrilege? Ask your uncle about sacrilege.

(To Newton)

My father told me much about you, that you are an anti-Trinitarian. He also told me that you had to have a special dispensation in the oath taking when you got your appointment at Cambridge. Do you think that I do not know why? How do you think the prelates of the Church of England would react if they knew that the great Sir Isaac Newton does not believe in the Holy Trinity: God, The Father; God, The Son; and God, The Holy Ghost? It was not so long ago that people in England were burned at the stake for your kind of religious beliefs.

(Newton gasps)

Sir Isaac, if you have my husband hanged, I will do everything in my power to reveal to the world your secrets.

(Newton looks at her in horror.)

Yes, Sir Isaac, all of them.

Scene 5

AT RISE: Newton is talking to the audience.

NEWTON

So you see how aggressive a woman Challoner's wife was. She left me dumfounded and speechless. I guess you are wondering about the things she said. First, there was the business of there being no women in my life. I have already spoken of that with you, except to admit that women make me nervous. This does not apply to my niece, Catherine. I feel comfortable around her. But then, we are related. Also, she is such a sweet person, to say nothing of her attractive appearance, which is such a delight to the eye.

As far as that dirty business about Fatio, that concerned one of my old protégés, Fatio de Dullier. He lives in France now, and I never hear from him. But I do not want to speak about him, at least right now; that time when I associated with him was a very difficult period for me.

I can talk about Challoner's wife's attacks on me concerning religion. I cannot reconcile the trinity with a belief in monotheism. They are divergent as far as I am concerned. However, do not get me wrong, I do believe in God as the Supreme Being. My difficulty comes from those presumptuous churchmen who have the audacity to think that God, in all his absolute perfection, would deign to cast his everlasting and immutable laws in something as imprecise and imperfect as the language of words. The only sermons that I can tolerate in church, if you will allow me the liberty of calling them sermons, are the musical, wordless ones of Bach. Those I understand and agree with.

I do have another problem which Madame Challoner did not touch on, probably because she is ignorant of it; namely these endless squabbles with other scientists about various matters. With Leibniz, of course, it is who should have primacy in the development of the Differential Calculus, he or I. With Hooke, it was over how much credit I should give to him in the development of the Laws of Motion. I remember that he wrote me a letter where he talked in some vague way about the Inverse Square Law which, of course, is such an important part of the Laws of Motion. But he was his usual vague, wordy self with little details and no mathematical precision. I got furious at him. I had thought of the Inverse Square Law myself, years before, but had not focused on it as I would later on. Hooke was a very acrimonious man, and I will never forget our last conversation.

Scene 6

AT RISE: Hooke has come to see Newton. They are alone.

NEWTON

Robert, I was under the impression that you would never come to my house again.

HOOKE

Do not make me eat crow, Isaac.

NEWTON

All right. What do you want?

HOOKE

I came to plead with you to make some mention of my name in the Principia. At least mention that I thought of the Inverse Square Law first.

NEWTON

You did not think of it first. When I received your letter in which you discussed it, I had already thought of it. And no, I can't prove it. It seemed rather obvious to me at the time and therefore I did not feel it was necessary to publicize it.

HOOKE

You never responded to my letter.

NEWTON

No, I did not. I only respond when it is worth my while.

HOOKE

Had you responded, I might have been involved in what you have done in developing the Laws of Motion of the planets.

NEWTON

You were not necessary. I did it by myself.

HOOKE

Isaac, you have consigned me to be a secondary player in the game of science. I will only be known for that minor result of mine in Elasticity. Why, Isaac?

NEWTON

Because you didn't offer anything that I needed.

HOOKE

You don't think much of my work, do you?

NEWTON:

You are not what I call competent.

HOOKE

May I ask why not?

NEWTON

I found your work of an ad hoc nature and mostly concerned with special cases. You don't look for general underlying principles.

HOOKE

We are all not as good as you, Isaac.

NEWTON

You mean that you don't work as hard as I do.

HOOKE

No, you have all those mathematical skills that I and most other scientists do not have. We cannot compete with you.

NEWTON

Then go and acquire those so-called mathematical skills.

HOOKE

I cannot. Not only do I find mathematics too difficult, I find it uninteresting. I cannot learn it easily.

NEWTON

You mean you don't want to put in the effort. You would rather spend your evenings prowling the streets of London looking for women. I work in the evenings. My work never stops.

HOOKE

Life should be more than work. Where is the reward if one is always working and never takes any time off to enjoy oneself?

NEWTON

Now you know, Robert, why you are a secondary player in the game of science.

HOOKE

Don't you ever take time off, Isaac? It is well known that you drink when you have finished working in the evening and want to unwind?

NEWTON

A little medicinal drinking to help me sleep does not detract from my work.

HOOKE

My name could have been added to the chain of names of Copernicus, Kepler, Galileo, and yours as those responsible for the derivation of the Laws of Motion of the planets. Instead of four names, there could have been five. I would be famous in the history of science.

NEWTON

If you want that so much than why don't you work harder?

HOOKE

There are other things in life besides work, Isaac.

NEWTON

You mean women.

HOOKE

Yes, I mean women. I have never been popular with women, Isaac. The few women that I could get to go to bed with me were never ones that I really wanted, but only those that were willing to sleep with me. I could never get a woman that I really desired. There was this actress once, who I use to go to see every night she performed. She was beautiful. Not only was her face lovely but she had this beautiful figure. And she would show it. During the performance she would take off most of her clothes and she was one of these women who looked better the fewer clothes she had on. She had this perfect taut, slithery body. When she moved, her skin would glisten and gleam with the play of light and shadow. Her legs were exquisite, narrow in the ankles, thicker through the calves, tapering again at the knees and with no sag in the thighs. Even her feet were beautiful. And her torso; it was magnificent with firm breasts and beautiful shapely curves everywhere. I used to wait backstage to see her when she would leave, always with some grandiose looking man, compared to whom I would be unnoticeable. One night she came out and there was no one there to meet her. I went up to her and introduced myself. It seemed like she had never heard the name of Robert Hooke. I could see from her polite but disdainful look that to her I was no more than a gray-headed, unprepossessing, middle-aged man. Had I been the famous Isaac Newton, her look would have been that of a woman in the presence of eminence and one very anxious to please.

NEWTON

I doubt that; women don't know the names of scientists. But why are you talking about this; I hear the rumors, and if it gets to somebody like me, it means it that everybody else has heard it, that at present, your women problems are solved. You are having, supposedly, a sexual relationship with your niece, despite the fact that to some people that is incest.

HOOKE

It is not incest. Doesn't the Law permit first cousins to marry?

NEWTON

But a niece is one step closer than a first cousin.

HOOKE

Isaac, I was failing when she came into my life. She brought me back to life. Actually, I had never been alive until she came along. She didn't bring me back to life; she made me come alive for the first time. She is the only woman I have ever been to bed with whom I was also in love with.

NEWTON

Robert, one of the reasons that you are not one of my favorite people is because of your dirty mouth.

HOOKE

I am sorry Isaac, but this relationship is the high point of my life.

NEWTON

Would you exchange this relationship for having your name added to the chain of names of Copernicus, Kepler, Galileo, and mine in the derivation of the Laws of Motion?

HOOKE

Why can't a man have both? Has it never happened in life that a man can have more than one thing? Why not have it all? Look at your mentor, Montagu. He was rich; he became President of the Royal Society; and, he was very popular with the ladies, as even your own niece can attest to.

NEWTON

Robert, will you never learn to control that filthy mouth of yours.

HOOKE

Isaac, it is common knowledge that your niece was involved with Lord Halifax.

NEWTON

I find your presence here in my house, spewing out your verbal garbage, more and more distressing.

HOOKE

Isaac, is it possible that your hostility toward me has something to do with my having a relationship with my niece and you wanting to have one with yours, but not being able to bring it about? Your niece and mine are very similar in many ways. They are both young, beautiful, and well-disposed to their respective uncles; and, furthermore, we never saw them till they were grown and hence do not think of them as family.

NEWTON

I could never do with my niece what you do with yours.

HOOKE

But do you want to?

NEWTON

No, I do not want to; it would be unnatural.

HOOKE

Nothing that man does is unnatural: the Pharaohs of Egypt used to marry their sisters.

NEWTON

That's disgusting; besides, women are of no concern to me.

HOOKE

No, do you not find your niece's presence here in your house a distinct blessing? Doesn't the room light up when she enters? Don't you find her conversation about the most mundane matters entrancing? Don't you hunger for her presence when she has been away for a while?

NEWTON

Yes, but that does not mean that I want to sleep with her like you do with your niece. How did your brother react when he found out that you were sleeping with his daughter?

HOOKE

My brother died before the relationship started.

NEWTON

And if he were alive what would he do to you if he found out.

HOOKE

My brother was more concerned with gambling than his daughter.

NEWTON

And what does your brother's widow say about your relationship with her daughter?

HOOKE

My brother left his wife and daughter in financial straits; I have helped them.

NEWTON

So you have bought your sister-in-laws acquiescence. How can you live with yourself?

HOOKE

And how will you live with yourself if that counterfeiter, Challoner, is hanged? At least nobody will die because of my misdoings. My niece has not been harmed. I am beginning to see signs that she is getting tired of being shackled to an old man and soon she will find a way to discard me. She will find herself a suitable husband who will take care of her and her mother and I will have been just an interlude in her life. While you, Sir Isaac Newton, on the other hand, might possibly have never had any interludes in your life.

NEWTON

And you, Hooke, will be no more than a minor player in the world of science with your publications that are full of words and more words, and poorly written ones at that, and most importantly contain little mathematics or real science. I hope this is the last time you will ever come to my house, you foul-mouthed reprobate.

Scene 7

AT RISE: Newton is talking to audience.

NEWTON

Hooke's talk of love started me thinking if I had ever loved anybody or anything, for that matter. There is one thing that I have loved in my life. I have loved deciphering the secrets of the universe; or, should I say that I have loved finding out the divine plan of God, at least, the plan as I see it.

God had set the planets in motion. But it was not a random motion. Everybody knew this because of the regularity of the motions. The moon encircles the earth once a month; the earth goes around the sun once a year. I set myself the goal of finding the secret of this regularity. Copernicus had recognized the fact that the earth was not fixed but rather moved around the sun. Kepler guessed the formulas for the Laws of Motion but could not derive them. Galileo came up with the idea of gravity. But then I carne along; studied the work of these giants; men who could think the unthinkable. Just imagine the reaction of the world to these men when they expressed the idea that the earth was not the center of the universe. We all know of the troubles that Galileo had with the Inquisition and how he was forced to recant. What I have done is to climb up and stand on the shoulders of these giants and reach out further than any of them and further than any other man had ever reached. I reached and I reached and I reached. Most men live their lives satisfying their own petty physical needs; I, on the other hand, have tried to rise above this and find some of the eternal truths that explain the regularity of the motions of the planets. These God given eternal truths are, of course, the Laws of Motion.

Of course as some of you might already know that because of pressure from the Royal Society which I and Hooke both belonged to, that I had to put Hooke's name in the Principia saying that he had discovered the Inverse Square Law independently. But I never forgave Hooke for his personal attacks on me. For revenge I never went to the Royal Society meetings until after he had died, so as to avoid ever seeing him again.

You are all probably wondering if I would have treated the great Leibniz differently than that second-rater Hooke. Leibniz was more my equal, but I assert that he did not discover the Differential Calculus before me; he just published first. Also, I always felt he was privy to some communications of mine to the Dutch scientist Huygens as well as others. But let us hear from Leibniz directly. This results from a secret visit of his to me in England which very few people know about, which I shall now tell you of.

Scene 8

AT RISE: Leibniz has come to see Newton. They are alone.

LEIBNIZ

Isaac Newton, I am very glad to see you. I never thought this meeting would take place.

NEWTON

It is nice to see you Herr Leibniz, it is interesting that our paths have never crossed before, considering that you have been to England several times before.

LEIBNIZ

Well, you were at Cambridge, and I would only visit London.

(Both men are silent for what seems to be a long time.)

NEWTON

You are staring at me Herr Leibniz.

LEIBNIZ

You are not as tall as I expected.

NEWTON

Why, how tall did you expect me to be?

LEIBNIZ

Oh, about ten feet tall.

NEWTON

You are not as tall as I expected.

LEIBNIZ

Why, what height did you expect me to be?

NEWTON

Oh, about nine feet tall.

LEIBNIZ

Touché, Isaac.

NEWTON

Herr Leibniz, I am surprised at how perfect your English is.

LEIBNIZ

Isaac, for many years, I have had to support myself by finding evidence that legitimizes the birth of bastard princelings whose wayward fathers happen to be rulers of small German principalities. It has been necessary for me to learn to speak many of the languages of Europe in order to do my job. But we have more important things to talk about.

NEWTON

Yes, we do.

LEIBNIZ

As I see it we have two things to discuss. One is who should get credit for the development of the Differential Calculus. The second is how much help did I get from correspondence with some of your fellow British mathematicians.

NEWTON

And don't forget your contacts with that Dutchman, Huygens, with whom I corresponded with and discussed my work in Calculus freely.

LEIBNIZ'

Yes, I remember Huygens showing me a letter of yours with some comments concerning Calculus in it.

NEWTON·

Well, do you feel that you got any benefit out of seeing the letter I sent to Huygens, which I do not think he should have shown you. That letter was meant for his eyes alone.

LEIBNIZ

Yes, I did see the letter that you sent Huygens.

NEWTON

You took advantage of me through Huygens.

LEIBNIZ

Haven't you done the same? Hooke has made it common knowledge that he wrote you about the Inverse Square Law many years before you proved the Laws of Motion.

NEWTON

I did not look over somebody's shoulder, breathing down his neck; I have this image of you drinking his and my blood like a vampire.

LEIBNIZ

That is very harsh, Isaac; science is the accumulation of bright ideas, each scientist building on the work of previous ones, like you proving Kepler's Laws.

NEWTON

It is not the same thing but I don't suppose you would understand that. So let us deal with the first issue you brought up; namely, who should get credit for the development of the Differential Calculus.

LEIBNIZ

Who is to say, Isaac, why does it have to be one of us? Could we not both receive credit? And remember we are not the only ones involved in the creation of the Differential Calculus. Do not forget the work of Fermat on Maxima and Minima and also the work of your old mentor Barrow. The only concession that I am willing to make is that you might have thought of it first but I was first to publish and that might be the critical thing.

NEWTON

Thank you for at least that admission Herr Leibniz. I did not expect you to admit that.

LEIBNIZ

You are welcome, Isaac, but I might not be so accommodating if we were not alone; otherwise, I would not be able to speak so freely.

NEWTON

You mean you would deny in public what you say to me in private.

LEIBNIZ

Let us say that I would be more circumspect if we had witnesses.

NEWTON

I thought so. Now tell me in private, how much of your work in the development of Differential Calculus can you attribute to little hints you might have gotten from your correspondence with other British mathematicians who know about my work and from my letter to Huygens which you read.

LEIBNIZ

Isaac, I don't think I can answer that question. Who is to say if any of the things I did in the Differential Calculus carne to me because of some revelation of yours given to me harmlessly or indirectly by one of your fellow British mathematicians or from your letter to Huygens? Certainly my notation is my own, since you don't even seem to use it, even though I feel it to be superior.

NEWTON

Yes, I agree your notation is very suggestive; it makes Differential Calculus seem more like ordinary calculations and seems to be the one most people use when they apply it. But I don't find your answer very satisfying.

LEIBNIZ

I know. I would not find my answer very satisfying either, but I cannot give you a better one. I do not feel that I ever purposely stole from you. I gathered ideas where I could and put everything together, just like you did with the writings of Copernicus, Kepler and Galileo.

NEWTON

All right, let us not discuss it anymore.

(After a long pause.)

LEIBNIZ

Isaac, are you aware of how much alike we are?

NEWTON

Alike? What do you mean by that?

LEIBNIZ

Besides our interest in mathematics and science, we have another common interest.

NEWTON

And what is that, Herr Leibniz?

LEIBNIZ

Religion!

NEWTON

Yes, I am interested in religion.

LEIBNIZ

Interested! I hear that you are obsessed with it.

NEWTON

I admit to spending a lot of time and effort reading and writing about religion.

LEIBNIZ

The word is that you do not believe in the Trinity.

NEWTON

I thought that I had kept that secret.

LEIBNIZ

I have a great sympathy for that view. However, my main concern is ecumenicalism. I feel that the division of Christianity into Catholicism and Protestantism with all the separate sects of the latter weakens Christianity.

NEWTON

I see we both have the typical mathematician's desire for there to be unity in all things.

LEIBNIZ

Yes, unity gives power through simplicity. I am sure that we, as mathematicians, with our need to abstract truth in the form of symbols, agree on something else about religion; namely, that religion seems to be hurt by its expression in word form because of the different interpretations of words that people have.

NEWTON

Those are my feelings exactly.

LEIBNIZ

Good, but there is one other thing I want to discuss before this meeting comes to an end.

NEWTON

Yes, what is that?

LEIBNIZ

Challoner!

NEWTON

Challoner, why would you want to discuss him?

LEIBNIZ

Sir Isaac, I want to know why you, the greatest scientist the world has ever known and possibly ever will know, yes, I admit it, - your work on the Laws of Motion and Gravity will change the world like no other scientist before or after will - can involve yourself in this execution of a petty criminal like Challoner?

NEWTON

Challoner is a willful man and has done things which I do not like.

LEIBNIZ

But whatever he has done, do you want your name, Isaac Newton, the man whose work will probably advance science more than the work of any other scientist, to be associated with such barbarism as the hanging of a minor criminal?

NEWTON

Would you say that if you were old, living from hand to mouth, and one day find that your life savings had depreciated to nothing because of currency crimes like those of Challoner. Besides, he has said things which have annoyed me very much.

LEIBNIZ

What things?

NEWTON

I can't talk about them.

LEIBNIZ

If there ever was a time to talk about it, now is the time, Isaac. You are talking about it at a meeting that never occurred with a person you never met; and, above all, you are talking about it with a person who is very much like you.

NEWTON

I shall not talk about them; besides, I do not think that we are so much the same.

LEIBNIZ

I assure you the differences are only superficial.

NEWTON

You must meet a lot of women at the various courts you spend your time at. I never meet any.

LEIBNIZ

Yes I meet a lot of women, being in court, but they mostly ignore me; and, if they don't ignore me they get bored with me very quickly. Isaac, there has never really been a woman in my life. (Pause.) Although, once I did propose to a woman. She never responded and after a while I lost interest. Mathematics, as you well know, is a jealous mistress.

NEWTON

But you seem to meet women. For me that's never the case.

LEIBNIZ

Has not a woman ever caught your fancy, Isaac?

NEWTON

Yes, there have been several, one in particular.

LEIBNIZ

Can you tell me about her?

NEWTON

I knew her before I went to Cambridge: a Miss Storer. She lived on a farm near to my mother's. She liked me; I liked her.

LEIBNIZ

And?

NEWTON

I went to Cambridge. When I returned a few years later, to avoid the Plague, which had finally reached Cambridge, she was married.

LEIBNIZ

That's it!

NEWTON

Yes, that's all I am going to say about it.

LEIBNIZ

Now you know why when you graduate college, you get a Bachelor's degree.

NEWTON

Very amusing. But not to change the subject, Herr Leibniz, I have a question to ask of you; it is rather delicate.

LEIBNIZ

Oh!

NEWTON

It is about me and one of my old protégés, Fatio de Duillier. What do they say about Fatio and me in Europe?

LEIBNIZ

The usual garbage that the mediocrities say about everyone who is superior to them in some way.

NEWTON

Tell me exactly!

LEIBNIZ

But Isaac, you cannot take seriously what guttersnipes say about you.

NEWTON

Tell me!

LEIBNIZ

Alright; they say that your relationship with Fatio was more than that of savant and protégé.

NEWTON

Do you believe that?

LEIBNIZ

No. But I did hear that you wanted him to come and live with you, and then broke off all contact with him very suddenly. What happened?

NEWTON

I invited him to come and live with me because I knew that he was in financial difficulties.

LEIBNIZ

But Fatio is a third rate mathematician; he should be working in his father's store or on his father's farm, whatever his father does, or at most teaching in a secondary school. Why would you concern yourself with somebody of so little promise?

NEWTON

There was something about him that intrigued me.

LEIBNIZ

But then why the sudden breaking off of all contact?

NEWTON

I don't know. In the midst of the exchange of letters between Fatio and me, in which we were discussing the possibility of him coming to stay with me, I, all of a sudden, got very depressed. This depression alternated with bouts of excruciating anxiety. It was during this period that I broke off contact with him. I cannot explain the depression or the anxiety. This period lasted for over a year and then the depression and the anxiety subsided.

LEIBNIZ

Was that the year of your depression that I hear about?

NEWTON

Yes, it was.

(After a long pause.)

LEIBNIZ

Isaac, there was a Fatio in my life. His name was Wilhelm Dillinger. But unlike Fatio who you broke with, he broke off contact with me when I refused to put him in my will. But, Isaac, these things are better not examined too closely. Thank God that your depression has passed.

NEWTON

Yes, I suppose you are right.

LEIBNIZ

Isaac, I shall leave you now.

NEWTON

I have the feeling that we will never see each other again.

LEIBNIZ

I have that same feeling, Isaac.

NEWTON

Goodbye, Herr Leibniz.

LEIBNIZ

Goodbye, Isaac.

Scene 9

At Rise: Newton is talking to the audience.

NEWTON

Leibniz was an interesting man. He was a strange combination of scholar and politician. However, he was not politician enough to get that German, who became King George III of England, to bring him to England from Germany when he became King. Leibniz certainly wished to come here. Maybe he knew too much about the genealogies of the court, including that of the King himself.

Leibniz was truthful in what he said about his relationships with women; they were, superficial. When he died, only his dog and male secretary came to his burial. It could be that the reason he wanted to come to England with King George so badly was that, despite our differences, he thought that I could have been a friend of his. In any case, if he had been able to come to England, the question of who had primacy in the development of Calculus might not have become so virulent. He was never the prime force in the controversy, but rather other German mathematicians carried the banner for him. I, for some reason, got very involved in this, helping other English mathematicians to write letters in the endless disputations. This became a national problem in that it became an argument of England versus Germany. It became so vitriolic that even though we English are cousins to the Germans, because of the intermixing due to endless Saxon invasions, I fear that England and Germany might possibly be enemies in future times.

You all probably wonder what ever happened to Amanda Taggert. She was the widow whom John Locke wanted me to meet. I can't believe how angry I got at him for this attempt to embroil me with women. He was only trying to help me. I apologized to him; and, I finally met this Amanda Taggert as you will now find out.

Scene 10

AT RISE: A Sunday evening. The widow Taggert
has come to see Isaac Newton.

NEWTON

Madam, who are you? How dare you barge into my study like
this? How did you get into my house?

AMANDA

My name is Amanda Taggert, and I dare to come here
because it is the only way it seems that I can see you. And, I
came in by the front door; it was open.

NEWTON

Where is my niece? She is always present when I have a
female visitor.

AMANDA

I know. That is why I came when I knew she would be out.

NEWTON

You purposely came here to see me when you knew I would
be alone. Why?

AMANDA

Because you hide behind your niece and the chance of my getting what I want would be much reduced if your niece were here.

NEWTON

What do you want from me?

AMANDA

Why did you not let John Locke arrange a meeting between us? Then I would not have had to be so forward as to come here without an invitation.

NEWTON

So you are the widow Taggert. I am not interested in meeting you, and I want you to leave my house immediately.

AMANDA

Why? Are you afraid of me? Do you think I have come here to hurt you?

NEWTON

I told Locke that I am not interested in women.

AMANDA

Are you not interested in women or are you afraid of them?

NEWTON

How dare you say that to me? I do not have to tolerate this.

AMANDA

Sir Isaac, I am considered to be very attractive by most men; my late husband, bless his soul, left me a very wealthy woman. Most men would be very anxious to make my acquaintance.

NEWTON

I do not happen to be one of them.

AMANDA

Are you sure of that?

NEWTON

You are very outspoken.

AMANDA

You have forced me to be so.

NEWTON

Alright, what do you want to say to me?

AMANDA

Do you find me attractive?

NEWTON

Why are you asking me this?

AMANDA

Do you find any woman attractive? Do you ever notice women? Do you know the difference between an attractive woman and one who is less favored?

NEWTON

Is it so important that a woman be attractive?

AMANDA

Sometimes, although it seems to not be important if one falls in love. Have you ever been in love, Sir Isaac? Do you know what it feels like?

NEWTON

Madam, why this inquisition?

AMANDA

Are you afraid to answer my question?

NEWTON

I don't know, but I have found myself obsessed with certain women, where I found myself always thinking about them.

AMANDA

Did you ever try to develop a relationship with any of these women?

NEWTON

No!

AMANDA

May I ask why not?

NEWTON

I don't know. I was busy with my work or they seemed not to be interested in me.

AMANDA

Or was it that you might have been afraid to approach them.

NEWTON

No! Why would I be afraid?

AMANDA

Because you were vulnerable to them, and they could hurt you.

NEWTON

Madam, I find this conversation very unpleasant.

AMANDA

Yes, I can see that you do. Also, it is very understandable that you should. But let me change the subject, if I may. Do you not notice anything familiar about me? We have crossed paths in the past. Do you not recognize me, Isaac?

NEWTON

You do look familiar to me.

AMANDA

Do you remember Brown's Tobacco shop in Cambridge?

NEWTON

Yes, I remember. No, it can't be. Were you that little girl - his daughter, I presume - who used to stare at me so intently when I would come into the store?

AMANDA

Yes, that was me, and I notice that you are doing now what you did then; namely, you avert looking into my eyes. We cannot connect with each other unless you somehow find the courage to look directly into my eyes. It is one of the ways men and women make contact with each other.

NEWTON

I don't know if I want to make contact with you.

AMANDA

Why don't you make contact first and then decide afterward if you want to?

NEWTON

Wouldn't it hurt your feelings if I made contact and then decided that I did not want to maintain contact?

AMANDA

Yes, but I would survive. Stop worrying about me, Isaac, maybe it is time that you worried about yourself.

NEWTON

Don't talk to me as if I were a child.

AMANDA

In some ways you are a child.

NEWTON

Am I so different than other men?

AMANDA

No, many men refuse to discuss certain things, especially concerning their feelings.

NEWTON

Can we discuss something else?

AMANDA

Well then, let us talk about science or mathematics. My father allowed me, unlike most women, to be educated. When I was I girl I had the finest tutors, and I know much about science and mathematics. I have even read the Principia and am probably the only woman in England who can make that claim.

NEWTON

But did you understand it?

AMANDA

There were parts of it that I could not follow and was hoping that you would explain those parts to me.

NEWTON

You are trying to disarm me and make me want to know you better.

AMANDA

Have I succeeded?

NEWTON

I don't know.

AMANDA

Let us go to another subject which I feel you will have less equivocal feelings about. I know about your problem with Challoner's wife, and I can help you with it.

NEWTON

How can you help me?

AMANDA

I can silence her.

NEWTON

How can you do that?

AMANDA

By telling her that I know that her own father, a minister, is a secret Unitarian and that if she persists in this inquisition of you, I will publicly expose her father.

NEWTON

I did not know that her father was a Unitarian. You are very clever, and I would appreciate your doing this for me.

AMANDA

I will expect something in return.

NEWTON

What?

AMANDA

The chance to intrude myself into your life. Yes, I know now you are feeling disturbed. Let us talk. I promise you I will not hurt you. Tell me, why there is no woman in your life?

NEWTON

How dare you ask me that question?

AMANDA

Because I am willing to help you and therefore feel entitled to ask you that question.

NEWTON

How come you don't ask me how I carne to discover the Laws of Motion to explain the motion of the planets?

AMANDA

Because I know the answer to that question.

NEWTON

You do? What is the answer?

AMANDA

Because you are the greatest scientific mind that England has ever produced.

NEWTON

Thank you for saying that. But are you trying to flatter me?

AMANDA

No, you are England's greatest mathematician, and you know it, but let us return to my original question. Why is there no woman in your life?

NEWTON

I don't know. Bad luck, I guess.

AMANDA

Did you love your mother?

NEWTON

Of course I loved my mother. What kind of question is that? Doesn't everybody?

AMANDA

I myself have never had any children, but I know how the difficulties of life are such that sometimes a mother can, unknowingly, hurt her children, even though she loves them very much.

NEWTON

What are you getting at?

AMANDA

Usually when a man has no women in his life, it is because he has or had a problem with his mother.

NEWTON

Nobody is perfect, why must a mother be so?

AMANDA

She doesn't have to be perfect; but she has a very powerful influence on the type of life that a son will live.

NEWTON

All right, I agree with that. So where are we in this discussion?

AMANDA

I cannot believe you are happy living the way you do.

NEWTON

No! Why not? I have my scientific work and my position at the Mint. My niece lives with me so I have company when I want it.

AMANDA

I sense a deep feeling of bitterness in you. I feel that is why you are so harsh as Warden of the mint. I cannot believe that you feel that the counterfeiter, Challoner, deserves to be hanged.

NEWTON

Let me tell you something about Challoner. He induced some cohorts of his to produce some counterfeit currency and then he turned them in for the reward.

AMANDA

Is that the reason he is to be hanged? Or is there no other reason?

NEWTON

What do you mean, other reason?

AMANDA

Something that has nothing to do with his crime.

NEWTON

What are you getting at?

AMANDA

Is there something personal between you and Challoner?

NEWTON

All right, there is something.

AMANDA

Tell me Isaac.

NEWTON

I am embarrassed to talk about it.

AMANDA

This will be our secret, I promise.

NEWTON

He humiliated me in public by saying that because I had no women in my life that I was not really a man.

AMANDA

Yes, that is not a very nice thing to say, and it says a lot about him. However, is that something to hang for?

NEWTON

Where is all this leading?

AMANDA

I still feel that you are not easy in your mind about your mother.

NEWTON

If you must know, my mother abandoned me when I was two years old.

AMANDA

What do you mean she abandoned you? Did she leave you in a basket on the steps of a church?

NEWTON

No, my father had died and she remarried. My stepfather, however, refused to have me live with them, and I had to go live with my grandparents.

AMANDA

That must have been very difficult for you. Did your grandparents love you and take good care of you?

NEWTON

They did love me, but they were old. My grandfather was always falling asleep in his chair and the ashes of his pipe would spill all over him. My grandmother would never hug me like my mother would when she came to visit me on Sundays to take me to church.

AMANDA

Were you angry with your mother for leaving you?

NEWTON

Yes, I was angry, very angry.

AMANDA

How angry?

NEWTON

I used to have thoughts of burning down the house where my mother and stepfather lived.

AMANDA

Have you never tried to forgive your mother? Maybe she did not have any choice.

NEWTON

Yes she did. We were not poor. She had the farm. She did not need to remarry in order to survive. She could have stayed with me or at least married a man who would have let me stay with her.

AMANOA

Isaac, a woman doesn't always have so many choices and chances. Your mother would never have done anything that she knew would hurt you.

NEWTON

Yes, I know that. What is going to be the end result of this conversation? How did we get into talking about my mother, and my telling you, a stranger, such private things about myself?

AMANDA

Isaac, you have to forgive your mother; otherwise you will not be able to let another woman into your life.

NEWTON

I have forgiven her.

AMANDA

That is not altogether true.

NEWTON

What do you mean by that? I said that I have forgiven her.

AMANDA

Do you ever find that the feeling of bitterness towards her returns with a force that surprises you?

NEWTON

Yes, it does, but how do you know that?

AMANDA

Sometimes it is easier to see things from the outside looking in than from inside looking out, like looking into a house at night when all the lights are on.

NEWTON

What else can you see?

AMANDA

I see why you have worked so hard to explain how the universe works.

NEWTON

Oh, have I really done that. I guess the Laws of Motion could be looked at that way. But what is the reason I have done this besides just scientific curiosity.

AMANDA

Curiosity would not have made you work the endless hours that it took to do what you did. Maybe the reason is that you did it to gain your mother's approval; you blamed yourself for having done something that she disapproved of to explain her leaving.

NEWTON

I don't understand. Why would I blame myself? I didn't do anything wrong.

AMANDA

When a child has to choose between blaming himself or his mother, he usually chooses to blame himself. Who could ever blame one's own mother?

NEWTON

I do not blame myself.

AMANDA

Are you sure?

NEWTON

Yes, I'm sure; at least I think I'm sure.

AMANDA

What will the scientific community think in years to come about the great Sir Isaac Newton spending so much of his energy and time on the Mint? They will wonder if the joy of scientific creation was not enough to satisfy his needs, or, will they see an undercurrent of fury which was never assuaged by the glories of science. Will not the world see the fury of a little boy aching at his mother's rejection of him and who never forgave her? Before it is too late, Isaac, you have to find a way to purge yourself of these feelings or you will go to your grave as a man who never came to terms with his past, accepted it, and went on from there.

NEWTON

Maybe you are right. I do want to get over this bitterness toward my mother which surges up for no reason at times and surprises me by its intensity, I hate having those feelings. I have fought against them, but I can never bury them completely. They keep recurring, and I am powerless to prevent these recurrences.

AMANDA

I will help you bury these feelings, Isaac.

NEWTON

How can you help me?

AMANDA

That is a woman's secret.

NEWTON

In any case, I am not used to letting women help me to do anything.

AMANDA

That is part of your problem.

NEWTON

Maybe it is too late for me to change certain things.

AMANDA

Does the world's greatest scientist want to give up on a problem without even trying to solve it? Can the solution of this problem be more difficult than discovering the Laws of Motion for the universe?

NEWTON

But I had a lot of help with that problem. There was Copernicus, Kepler, and Galileo.

AMANDA

Now you have me to help; I knew there was a reason why I worked so hard on the Principia. But before we start on your problem, I have a problem about something on page 74 of the third edition of the Principia.

NEWTON

Oh yes, I know about that; but the problem is due to a misprint. Do you want me to explain it to you?

AMANDA

Do you think I will understand the explanation, Isaac?

NEWTON

I hope so, Amanda; I truly do.

AMANDA

Isaac, do you realize you called me Amanda; that's the first time you've used my first name.

NEWTON

Well, you have been calling me Isaac.

AMANDA

So I have, Isaac.

(They both laugh; the lights go down; the curtain falls.)

ONE PLUS ONE
EQUALS ONE

Characters

Joan

Ken

At rise: Joan and Ken are in a bare hut halfway up a Swiss mountain in the Alps. A severe storm is in progress.

Ken

I've never been on a climb like this before.

Joan

Tell me about it. The storm makes this the worst climb I've ever been on.

Ken

Boy, I'm glad we got to this hut.

Joan

Yeah, I couldn't have gone much more without a break.

Ken

How much more do we have to go to reach the top?

Joan

I think that we're a little more than halfway up.

Ken

By the way, my name is Ken, Kenneth Lane. I'm sorry that I didn't introduce myself when we started out.

Joan

I understand. Serious rock climbing has a way of eliminating small talk. I'm Joan.

Ken

What's happened to our guide?

Joan

He went outside to check the conditions.

Ken

This storm came up rather suddenly.

Joan

Yes, this is very freakish for this time of the year.

Ken

Did you notice how icy that last pitch was?

Joan

Yes, I noticed.

Ken

Without you belaying me, I don't think I would have made it.

Joan

No, you would have made it.

Ken

Listen to that wind.

Joan

I hear it.

Ken

The cliff face above us seems awfully exposed.

Joan

It is. I don't think we can continue in this wind.

Ken

Does that mean we have to go back down?

Joan

The guide is checking that right now.

Ken

What would we do, God forbid, if the guide had an accident and got hurt or disappeared?

Joan

Stop worrying. He knows this mountain very well. He told me that he has led more than fifty climbs up it.

Ken

Yeah, but has he ever led a climb when the conditions were this bad?

Joan

I get the impression that he has never been on the mountain when it was this bad.

Ken

Damn, it's freezing in here. Why is there no heat in this hut?

Joan

It's only meant to be a temporary resting place to get out of the wind.

Ken

I can see that. There are no supplies or sleeping bags.

Joan

There's a supply hut just over the top that we would hit on the way down the backside of the mountain.

Ken

Why didn't they make this a supply hut, too?

Joan

Because this side is too steep to have brought up a lot of stuff.

Ken

But they got this hut up here.

Joan

Would you stop it, for God's sake? Just calm down.

Ken

Sorry. I guess I'm a little nervous.

Joan

Relax. Let's just wait till the guide returns.

Ken

I noticed that you and he were speaking German just before he went outside to scout the conditions.

Joan

Yes. His English isn't very good.

Ken

I thought his English sounded okay before we started climbing.

Joan

Well, maybe because of the stress, he reverted back to his native language.

Ken

Stress! You mean he's worried?

Joan

He's a good climber and a good leader. He treats this mountain with the respect that it deserves.

Ken

What does that mean?

Joan

It means that he's a professional and tries to be very careful. Now stop bothering me.

Ken

I'm sorry.

Joan

Pardon me for saying this, but I don't think you've had enough experience to be on a climb like this.

Ken

Well, why didn't the guide say something about that when we started out?

Joan

Oh, there are a couple of reasons for that. For one, you were the third person on the rope, so he couldn't see you on the climb as well as I could. I guess since I'm more experienced than you, I should have been number three, but usually they don't let a woman be last on a climb.

Ken

And what's the second reason?

Joan

Well, this is his living, and you would have been okay if the weather hadn't gotten so bad.

Ken

You mean our guide cut a few corners.

Joan

Maybe. But doesn't everybody? Haven't you ever driven home from a party or a bar when you've had too much to drink?

Ken

But that is a little different.

Joan

Oh, is it? Suppose you had an accident driving under the influence and somebody besides yourself got hurt.

Ken

I don't think the situations are the same.

Joan

Really! I disagree.

Ken

All right, so maybe the situations are similar, but it still seems that the guide should have considered the possibility of bad weather. There must have been some indication.

Joan

No, there wasn't. In the mountains, the weather can change instantaneously.

Ken

I don't like this.

Joan

Hey, you signed up for this climb.

Ken

Yes, I did. I knew this climb was at the outer limits of my skill.

Joan

So why did you sign up?

Ken

I had a couple of reasons.

Joan

May I ask what they were?

Ken

Sometimes when I hit a snag in my work, it clears up when I go on a climb like this.

Joan

You mean you get some help from your subconscious.

Ken

Yes. That's exactly what it is.

Joan

Wouldn't going on a hike work just as well?

Ken

No. Unless there is some anxiety involved, it doesn't seem to help.

Joan

What kind of work do you do?

Ken

I'm a crystallographer.

Joan

A what?

Ken

A crystallographer. I determine the structure of molecules.

Joan

What? Is that important?

Ken

It's hard to explain it to somebody who doesn't have a technical background.

Joan

I am a college graduate.

Ken

All right, it could lead to the cure for cancer.

Joan

What did you say?

Ken

It could lead to the cure for cancer.

Joan

I don't see the connection between the structure of molecules and the cure for cancer.

Ken

Cancer is the result of the growth of certain kinds of cells. There are treatments that can destroy these cells. Unfortunately, these treatments have bad side effects, like a lot of chemotherapy. But cells are made up of molecules. By determining the structure of the molecules in the cells, it is possible to create a drug that destroys the cancer cells without the bad side effects.

Joan

Have there been any notable successes with this approach?

Ken

Yes. A medication has been developed for treating congestive heart failure that works very well without any downside, unlike the old treatment of digitalis that is very toxic.

Joan

I would think that to do this kind of work, you would have to be a biologist.

Ken

Most of the people at the institute where I work are biologists. But the really important work is done by crystallographers.

Joan

Do the biologists agree with that?

Ken

On the surface no, but down deep I think that they do.

Joan

How do you know that?

Ken

Well, my boss is a biologist, and even though I think he feels threatened by my knowledge of crystallography, he still works very closely with me and wants to know everything that I do. Sometimes he spends all day at my side, asking me to explain things.

Joan

Tell me; are you close to finding the cure for cancer?

Ken

We've developed some medicines that allow us to put some cancers into indefinite remission.

Joan

But remission is not a cure.

Ken

That's the next step, and we learn a lot from the remission.

Joan

Well, I wish you luck. I just lost a close friend to cancer, and it was terrible.

Ken

I'm sorry.

Joan

You said there were a couple of reasons why you came on this climb.

Ken

The second one is a little embarrassing for me to talk about.

Joan

I think that since we are halfway up a mountain in a hut, waiting out a storm, you can tell me.

Ken

I feel foolish.

Joan

And I feel annoyed.

Ken

Okay, I'll tell you. Besides the benefit to my work, I was hoping to meet an attractive woman. A lot of good-looking women do this kind of thing.

Joan

Seems like a lot of trouble just to meet a woman. Don't you meet women back home?

Ken

I don't have good luck with women.

Joan

No! Why not? You make a good living, you're not bad looking, and you're not what I would call shy.

Ken

Well, usually, if I like her, she doesn't like me, or vice versa.

Joan

Doesn't everybody have that problem?

Ken

Maybe, but I don't think to the degree that I have.

Joan

Could it be that you just don't try hard enough?

Ken

What do you mean?

Joan

It seems that in my experience, when a man doesn't get a woman he wants, it's because he didn't want her badly enough.

Ken

It does seem that sometimes I give up too quickly.

Joan

Why do you think that happens?

Ken

Well, one reason is that my work seems to interfere. I feel that I have to solve some problem that comes up before I feel that I will be ready to make an all-out effort for a particular woman.

Joan

Is it your work, or are you just finding an excuse not to get involved?

Ken

What are you, a psychologist?

Joan

No, I'm just a woman with women's intuition.

Ken

Why would I not want to get involved?

Joan

You're a smart man. I'm sure you'll figure it out.

Ken

Thank you, doctor. Send me your bill.

Joan

Tell me something, Ken. Do you like me?

Ken

What did you say?

Joan

Do you find me attractive?

Ken

Well, you are a very good-looking woman.

Joan

Do I appeal to you?

Ken

Well, now that you mention it, I think so.

Joan

You think so. You don't know.

Ken

All right, I find you very attractive.

Joan

I noticed you staring at me in the cocktail lounge the other night.

Ken

You did! You noticed me?

Joan

You kept staring at me. It was hard not to notice it.

Ken

I couldn't keep my eyes off you while you were dancing. It was like you and your partner were performing.

Joan

Why didn't you ask me to dance?

Ken

I'm not a good dancer.

Joan

Is that the only reason?

Ken

Well, I thought you were with your boyfriend.

Joan

Boyfriend! I don't even remember his name. I just met him that evening in the lounge.

Ken

But you seemed so comfortable with each other. I thought surely you both were involved.

Joan

That was just good cocktail lounge interaction skills. You gave up too quickly.

Ken

The story of my life!

Joan

So what did you do, just end up getting drunk that night?

Ken

I think I did. But what's wrong with that. I wasn't going to be driving anywhere that night. Besides, I thought I'd catch you another time.

Joan

A chance encounter, perhaps!

Ken

Yeah, I figured our paths would cross when it would have been easier for me to meet you.

Joan

Oh, my God! Did you sign up for this climb because of me?

Ken

What?

Joan

I asked you if you signed up for this climb because of me.

Ken

Well, uh...

Joan

Well, what? Did you sign up for this climb because you somehow knew that I was going to be on it?

Ken

I think so.

Joan

Another "I think so!" Don't you know, or are you afraid to admit it?

Ken

All right, I signed up because I knew that you were going to be on this climb.

Joan

How did you know?

Ken

I was standing by the sign-up board when you put your name down.

Joan

And then you just put down your name also?

Ken

Yes.

Joan

Didn't it bother you that this climb was maybe a little beyond your skill and experience level?

Ken

I'm tired of always being afraid.

Joan

"Faint heart never won fair maiden."

Ken

Something like that.

Joan

Maybe you should have just asked me to dance.

Ken

Would you have said yes?

Joan

Probably not.

Ken

May I ask why not?

Joan

A woman doesn't need a reason to say no, just to say yes.

Ken

Come on, there must be a reason why you would say no.

Joan

Well, if you must know, you're not my type.

Ken

Why, am I not your type?

Joan

You have that innocent look.

Ken

I hate it when a woman says that to me, especially if it's one that I like.

Joan

I'm sorry.

Ken

By the way, didn't you say that if a man really wants a woman, he gets her?

Joan

I didn't say that exactly. Besides, you shouldn't expect anything in life to be that simple. Your work isn't.

Ken

Oh, you're quick.

Joan

A woman has to be quick. It's one of the necessary qualities in the eternal battle of the sexes.

Ken

It's been a while since the guide went out.

Joan

Yes, it has.

Ken

By the way, just before the guide left, when you and he were talking German, I noticed you both seemed upset.

Joan

You noticed that?

Ken

Yes, I did.

Joan

You don't understand German?

Ken

No. For my Ph.D., I used French and FORTRAN for my two languages.

Joan

FORTRAN!

Ken

Yes. Now that we are in the computer age, a computer language can be one of the two languages you need for a degree, FORTRAN being one of the popular computing languages.

Joan

I majored in German in college.

Ken

So tell me, why were you and the guide upset?

Joan

Can't you guess?

Ken

Something about this freak storm and the bad conditions?

Joan

Yes.

Ken

Well...

Joan

Well, what?

Ken

Can't you be more specific?

Joan

Isn't it obvious?

Ken

You mean we're in trouble?

Joan

Of course we're in trouble.

Ken

How much trouble?

Joan

Serious trouble. If conditions stay this bad, we can't continue on up to the top to the easy route down the backside.

Ken

So we go back down.

Joan

You noticed how icy it had become on the last pitch.

Ken

Yes. We talked about that.

Joan

Are you aware it is easier to climb up than it is to climb down?

Ken

Why can't we rappel down?

Joan

In this wind, it would be impossible, even if we had enough rope, which we don't.

Ken

So what are you saying?

Joan

The guide told me that unless conditions improve rapidly, he can only take one of us down with him.

Ken

This is what you were talking about when you and he were speaking in German before?

Joan

Yes. He realized that I was the more experienced climber and didn't want to upset you.

Ken

So if he can only take one of us down, what happens to the other?

Joan

When he gets down, he'll try to get a rescue party to come up for the one left behind.

Ken

Try!

Joan

Yes. Try!

Ken

But isn't there a law in Switzerland that says that every effort must be made to rescue a climber in trouble?

Joan

That doesn't mean rescuers have to commit suicide.

Ken

I don't understand. If he can take one down, why can't he take two?

Joan

Essentially, to get one of us down, he'd have to lower us bit by bit on belay.

Ken

Well, why couldn't he do that with both?

Joan

Hey, look, do you think he wants to leave one of us here? He can only handle one of us in that situation.

Ken

But it's getting late. There's no way a rescue party could get up here before dark.

Joan

That's right.

Ken

But then one of us would be here all night and probably freeze to death.

Joan

Now you know why he was upset before.

Ken

What about the guide going down by himself? Couldn't he do that quickly enough to bring a rescue party before dark?

Joan

I asked him that.

Ken

And!

Joan

He can move almost as fast with one of us as he can by himself. Also, he doesn't want to leave both of us up here.

Ken

Why not?

Joan

Because he knows what he's doing.

Ken

You mean it would look a lot better if he can save one of us than if he goes down by himself and runs the risk of being accused of abandoning us.

Joan

No. He would rather lose one than two.

Ken

So I guess that means you go and I stay.

Joan

No. He wants us to choose who goes with him.

Ken

Well, you, of course.

Joan

Why? Because I'm a woman.

Ken

Yes.

Joan

Are you a male chauvinist pig?

Ken

No.

Joan

Haven't you heard of the Women's Movement?

Ken

What are you getting at?

Joan

You should go down with the guide and I stay behind.

Ken

Why?

Joan

Because of what you do.

Ken

You mean my work.

Joan

Yes.

Ken

What do you do?

Joan

I spend my father's money and rock climb.

Ken

Why do you rock climb?

Joan

For the thrill of it.

Ken

The thrill!

Joan

Yes. You climb to get over blocks in your work. I climb for thrills. Do you know what I mean by thrills?

Ken

How dare you!

Joan

No. How dare *you*. You think you should let me go because I'm a woman.

Ken

You mean I should go down because my work is so important.

Joan

Yes.

Ken

But how could I live with myself?

Joan

God, you are innocent.

Ken

Stop that.

Joan

All right, there is another reason why I want you to go down with the guide.

Ken

What reason is that?

Joan

Can't you imagine any other good reason for my not wanting to go down instead of you?

Ken

Tell me, for God's sake.

Joan

It's very personal.

Ken

I would think we're beyond worrying about what is personal.

Joan

My last boyfriend tested HIV positive.

Ken

What about you? Did you test positive?

Joan

I'm still waiting for the minimum time to be up before I can be tested with certainty.

Ken

You know, it's not certain that you would have caught it from him.

Joan

A woman catches it from a man a lot easier than a man from a woman.

Ken

Even if you test positive, there's still hope. My institute has a whole department working on AIDS. One of the other crystallographers thinks he has a drug that works better as a treatment than any of the drugs now used.

Joan

What about a cure?

Ken

Not yet. But look, we've cured polio, TB, small pox, diphtheria. We've gone to the moon. It's only a matter of time.

Joan

I don't have any time.

Ken

Even if the worst is true, you have several years.

Joan

Do you know what it's like to die of AIDS? You waste away slowly, bit by bit. Do you think I want to go through that? You remember that girl who caught it from her dentist? They showed her on television, periodically, as she wasted away. Wouldn't you rather die quickly from freezing all in one night than slowly over a period of years?

Ken

But you're not sure you'll get AIDS.

Joan

I can't take the chance.

Ken

Joan there's something I have to tell you.

Joan

What?

Ken

This is hard for me to say.

Joan

Just say it.

Ken

Joan, I love you.

Joan

You liked my looks on the dance floor, and now you love me?

Ken

Yes.

Joan

If you love me, you would not want me to suffer.

Ken

But I don't want to lose you.

Joan

You'd rather I die in agony?

Ken

I don't know what to say.

Joan

Don't say anything.

Ken

But I've got to say something.

Joan

You could say that if we both make it down, you'd want to make love to me.

Ken

Yes, I would.

Joan

Even if I test positive?

Ken

Yes.

Joan

Are you sure?

Ken

Absolutely!

Joan

You're not just saying that?

Ken

No.

Joan

Maybe being innocent isn't all that bad.

Ken

Please don't start that again.

Joan

I think I hear the guide coming.

Ken

I think you're right.

Joan

If conditions have improved and we can continue up to the top, he'll come in; otherwise, he'll just knock.

Ken

Then what?

Joan

The one that we've agreed to go down with him will go out.

Ken

He will accept that?

Joan

Yes.

Ken

You worked this out with him when you were speaking German with him before he went out to check the conditions?

Joan

Yes. We didn't want to upset you.

Ken

I understand.

Joan

I'm sorry that we worked behind your back.

Ken

How will he know that I didn't just knock you out and walk out when he knocks?

Joan

He knows what kind of person you are.

Ken

You mean I have that innocent look.

Joan

No more of that, please. Say goodbye now, just in case he knocks.

Ken

Can't I say good luck?

Joan

No. I will be satisfied with nothing less than a goodbye.

Ken

I always have trouble saying goodbyes.

Joan

I know, but say it.

Ken

All right. Goodbye.

Joan

Goodbye. Oh, and one more thing.

Ken

What's that?

Joan

Work very hard. Work very hard.

Ken

I always do.

HYPATIA

A One Act Play

by

Arthur Ziffer

Characters

Hypatia

Theon, Hypatia's father

Raphael, a Jew

Cyril, a churchman

Scene 1

At rise: Hypatia and Theon talking in the
year 415 AD in Alexandria, Egypt.

Theon

I am sorry that I brought you up to be a scholar, Hypatia. I fear that you will never marry and give me grandchildren.

Hypatia

Father, I would not be happy in the role of most women, just being a wife and a mother.

Theon

Couldn't you be, besides a scholar, a wife and a mother?

Hypatia

That seems to not be a possibility; all my thoughts are concerned with mathematics and philosophy.

Theon

But if you had a husband and children you would have thoughts of them besides mathematics and philosophy. What about the Jew Raphael? He seems to be the kind of man that would allow you to do mathematics and philosophy besides being a wife and a mother.

Hypatia

I don't deny that he is an attractive man and if I had to marry somebody, it would be somebody like him.

Theon

Also he is wealthy and powerful and could protect you. I fear that you will get into trouble with your outspoken manner. You have antagonized Cyril and now that he is archbishop of Alexandria you could be in great danger.

Hypatia

Alexandria is, after Rome and Constantinople, the largest and most advanced city in the two empires; free speech is not against the law here.

Theon

But Cyril has eyes for you even though he is clergy and everything you say against religion inflames him.

Hypatia

I thought clergy were supposed to takes vows of celibacy.

Theon

Here in the Eastern Empire that is not the rule as it is becoming in the Western Empire.

Hypatia

That's what bothers me about Christianity, the differences, like that between the Arians and the Athenasians, each with different beliefs and rules. The Athenasians believe that the figure of Jesus is equal to God and the Arians believe he is less than equal to God. I have great difficulty with that.

Theon

Saying these things is what is getting you into trouble. Besides, I see the way Cyril looks at you; you would do well to avoid him and not talk about religion, just concern yourself with mathematics and philosophy.

Hypatia

But father, philosophy includes religion. To me belief in the ideas of Plato is as much a religion as Christianity.

Theon

Not to Cyril and his followers. To him belief in the ideas of Plato and not Christianity is heresy. I fear that if Cyril doesn't get his way with you, he will get you charged, convicted and punished as a heretic. Think of how they punish heretics here in Alexandria.

Hypatia

But if as you say Cyril wants me so badly, would he allow me to be punished as a heretic?

Theon

Don't say that Hypatia. You seem to have never experienced love and don't understand how men react when they are denied.

Hypatia

Father, I will think about what you say, but I must leave you to give my lecture at the Library.

Theon

That's another thing that frightens me, your connection with the Library. Many people feel that it is a repository of dangerous materials, writings that should have been suppressed years ago. That alone could get you into trouble.

Hypatia

The great Library of Alexandria is known the world over and is sacred to many people. Lecturing there might be the best way for me to protect myself. But I must leave you now; I am late for my lecture today.

Scene 2

At rise: Hypatia and Raphael later that day.

Raphael

Hypatia I love you. Please marry me.

Hypatia

I appreciate your sentiments Raphael, but I don't love you.

Raphael

I never heard you use the word love, Hypatia; I didn't think you knew what it meant.

Hypatia

Just because I have never been in love doesn't mean I don't know what it is all about. Also, I love mathematics and philosophy.

Raphael

That's not the same thing.

Hypatia

To me it is.

Raphael

Hypatia, I fear for you. Alexandria is seething with religious factions. Also, now that Cyril is archbishop you are in great danger because of your being so outspoken.

Hypatia

My father thinks that I am in danger because of Cyril's desire for me, even if he is a clergyman.

Raphael

I agree with your father. Marry me and we will go to Jerusalem where you will be safe.

Hypatia

I could never leave the great city of Alexandria and go to a backwater like Jerusalem.

Raphael

Then we can go to Babylon which has many Jews and is a prosperous and culturally advanced city like Alexandria.

Hypatia

Can we go even if I don't marry you?

Raphael

Yes, of course. Besides if we spent more time together, I know that you would grow to love me.

Hypatia

You are an attractive man and have great understanding. But what about the fact that I am not Jewish?

Raphael

That would not be a problem for me. I am old enough so that my parents would not disapprove of my marrying whom I choose.

Hypatia

And what about the fact that I could never believe in Judaism just like I can't believe in Christianity?

Raphael

Judaism is different than Christianity; there is no creed to believe in for Judaism.

Hypatia

Is that true for all the Jewish sects? As I remember from my reading of Jewish history, you have the Pharisees, the Sadducees, and the Essenes.

Raphael

You seem to know a lot about the Jews for an unbeliever. To answer your question, there were and are differences in belief between the various sects of the Jews. For example, in the time of Jesus Christ, some of the Pharisees liked the ideas of Christ, while the Sadducees were against Christ because of his feelings toward the Temple moneychangers.

Hypatia

Then why in the New Testament are the Pharisees blamed for the death of Christ?

Raphael

This came about because with the destruction of the Temple in 70 AD, the Sadducees who were guardians of the Temple disappeared, and since the Gospels were written after the destruction of the Temple, the Gospel writers picked the remaining major sect of the Jews, the Pharisees, to be responsible for the death of Christ. This also had the benefit of differentiating the Jews from the Christians so that Christianity was less offensive to the Romans.

Hypatia

Why was it necessary to differentiate the Jews from the Christians?

Raphael

The Jews were always causing trouble for the Romans in Palestine. There was a second revolt, besides the one from 66-70 AD, in 132 to 135 AD, the so called Bar Kockba rebellion, which cost so many Roman lives that when Hadrian the Roman emperor at that time visited Palestine, he omitted from his letter to the Roman Senate the usual "I and the Legions are well." Also, during the second revolt against the Romans, the Christians did not fight as Jews as they did during the first rebellion.

Hypatia

And why was that?

Raphael

The spiritual leader of the Jews, Rabbi Akiba who was alive during the first rebellion, and saw how the Jews could not help their factionalism from hurting them in their fight against the Romans, decided to proclaim the Jewish leader Simon Bar Kockba the Messiah in the hopes that it would unify the Jews in their fight against the Romans. This, of course, was the one thing the Christians could not accept and therefore would not fight with the Jews against the Romans.

Hypatia

What an interesting history you Jews have; I could marry you just to be part of such a group. By the way, what do you mean there is no creed for the Jews?

Raphael

It means that besides believing in the one God, the only thing you have to do Is follow the endless rules and regulations that we follow, none of which I think would be a problem for you.

Hypatia

You mean like not eating pork.

Raphael

Yes and a few more.

Hypatia

Being a vegetarian would make not eating pork easy. How many other rules and regulations are there?

Raphael

Many, but let's get married and discuss these at leisure.

Hypatia

You're very convincing; let me think about it.

Scene 3

At rise: Hypatia and Cyril still later that day.

Hypatia

Why have you had me brought here?

Cyril

Because now that I am Archbishop, I have the power to do so and I wanted to do it.

Hypatia

What is it that you want from me?

Cyril

You know what I want.

Hypatia

But why me? You could have any woman that you want. Although I thought Christian clergy were supposed to be celibate.

Cyril

That rule has still not been officially promulgated, especially here in the Eastern Empire.

Hypatia

But there are few priests who are married. So do you just want me to cohabit with you, or would you be willing to give up your position as archbishop to marry me?

Cyril

You mean if I left the clergy to marry you, you would be willing.

Hypatia

You know, Raphael has asked me to marry him.

Cyril

You would marry a Jew rather than me.

Hypatia

I haven't said yes to him, just that I would think about it.

Cyril

You know most of the Jews have been expelled from Alexandria.

Hypatia

I can't believe you did this; won't this be a problem in the commerce and trade of Alexandria?

Cyril

No, we did not have the Jews killed; we just expropriated their property unless they converted. Since many Jews converted, that meant they could remain in Alexandria and stay involved in what they are good at, namely commerce.

Hypatia

In any case I don't want to marry anyone. I am married to mathematics and philosophy.

Cyril

You don't have to marry me; I just want you to live with me.

Hypatia

What is it about me that makes you want me so?

Cyril

You are very beautiful.

Hypatia

There are many beautiful women in Alexandria.

Cyril

But none as beautiful as you.

Hypatia

I can't believe that.

Cyril

Believe it Hypatia; I have looked at lots of women. I haven't seen one that compares with you.

Hypatia

What is there about me that you find so attractive?

Cyril

Everything, especially the way you walk and move. I have been to your lectures at the Library and studied you. To me, you are physical perfection.

Hypatia

You are very flattering.

Cyril

Also, when you lecture you are wearing some light flimsy garb that shows every detail of your beautiful body. Why did you not cover yourself more? Maybe I wouldn't have become so entranced with you.

Hypatia

I am sorry; I didn't realize I was provoking you.

Cyril

Well you did and now it is too late to erase the provocation.

Hypatia

I am sorry, but I am married to mathematics and philosophy.

Cyril

You could still do your mathematics and philosophy and live with me.

Hypatia

It doesn't work that way. A person can only be married to one thing.

Cyril

But you say you are married to two things already; namely, mathematics and philosophy.

Hypatia

They can be thought of as one thing.

Cyril

I don't believe that. When you talk about the Astrolabe and the Hydroscope, I can understand that that is mathematics. But when you talk about Plato's philosophy like it is a religion, then you are no longer in the realm of mathematics. Furthermore, you say that Plato's philosophy is better than Christianity. To some this is heresy.

Hypatia

Are you referring to one of your underlings known as Peter the Reader?

Cyril

Yes, him among others. He is a very violent man. He wants all the Jews killed rather than just having their property expropriated and expelled from Alexandria like the moderate faction wants.

Hypatia

I hope you will always be able to keep him in check.

Cyril

If you were living with me, you would not have to worry about him.

Hypatia

Suppose I told you that I only want to have physical relations with women. My experiences with men have not been as satisfying as my relations with women.

Cyril

That's because you probably were not in love with any of the men.

Hypatia

Yes that's true.

Cyril

I'm sure that if you lived with me you would fall in love with me and we could reach some mutually satisfactory accommodation.

Hypatia

How do you know that I would fall in love with you?

Cyril

Because I would make you. I think I know what has to be done with you in order to make this happen.

Hypatia

You're frightening me.

Cyril

I know but it has to be done and it is for your good as well as mine which I think you realize.

Hypatia

I must go now but I will think about what you have said.

Scene 4

At rise: the next day with Raphael
and Theon talking together.

Raphael

I could not save your daughter.

Theon

They did terrible things to her.

Raphael

I don't think we Jews ever do such horrible things.

Theon

Don't you have four ways of executing people: stoning, drowning, beheading, and by fire? Isn't death by fire as bad as what they did to my daughter? Are you Jews any better?

Raphael

Yes, it does say in the Old Testament that those are the four ways of execution.

Theon

So!

Raphael

But we Jews rarely execute anybody. In order to execute anybody there have to be two witnesses who have to affirm that they told the guilty person that they were committing a capital crime and that they still persisted in doing the bad deed. In fact the Sanhedrin which has been designated as the killing Sanhedrin only allowed one execution.

Theon

How was the person killed?

Raphael

As I remember it was by stoning. This is not to be found in the Old Testament but in the Talmud.

Theon

The Talmud! How does that differ from the Old Testament?

Raphael

The Old Testament is the written law and the Talmud is the oral law. It spells out the details that amplify the Old Testament and includes much of the discussions that the Rabbi's had about things in the written law.

Theon

I wish Hypatia had married you and gone off to Babylon with you.

Raphael

So do I.

Theon

She was almost convinced of doing so.

Raphael

I didn't know.

Theon

At some point she was just about to go to you but then she thought it would be cowardly. She didn't want to be a coward like her father.

Raphael

Don't be too hard on yourself. Most people are cowards.

Theon

Who was responsible for her death?

Raphael

It was Peter the Reader.

Theon

Didn't Cyril try to stop it?

Raphael

I don't think he had a chance. Peter and his underlings were too quick for him.

Theon

Did you see how they killed her?

Raphael

No I didn't; I got there too late.

Theon

I was told that they took her out of a carriage she was riding in and brought her into a church where they stripped her naked and then tortured her to death.

Raphael

Try not to think about it.

Theon

What should I do now? It's terrible to outlive your children. I have no other family.

Raphael

Come with me and I will take care of you like the son-in-law I wanted to be.

Theon

Thank you! You are so kind. But I don't feel like I can go on living. I wish my wife were still alive or that we had had more than one child. I'd have something to live for. I don't even have any brothers or sisters.

Raphael

Hypatia would want you to survive and do your good deeds for others like you have always done.

Theon

All right, I will try for Hypatia's sake.

About the Author

Arthur Ziffer has been writing plays for about thirty years and publishing them for about ten years. He has published eight books of plays (some with only one play in it) and this book will be his ninth. The previous eight are as follows.

First was a book containing a play about the mathematician Isaac Newton with title *On the Shoulders of Giants*. This was co-authored with Herbert Hauptman, the first mathematician to win the Nobel Prize. (John Nash of *A Beautiful Mind* was the second). He won it in 1985 in Chemistry since there is no prize in mathematics.

The second book had the title *One Act Plays* which contained the plays with titles: *Countertransference, One Plus One Equals One, Mothers, Malcolm,* and *Mal. Mothers* can be performed with six women. *Malcolm* is a monologue for a man. *Mal* is an analogous monologue for a woman. The third book had the title *Two Act Plays* which contained the plays with titles: *Redemption* and *Death of a Psychiatrist.* Book number four contained two plays with titles: *Countertransference* and *Retribution.* Books number five, seven, and eight have respective titles: *Masada Revisited, Masada Revisited II,* and *Masada Revisited III.* All three are plays about the famous incident in Jewish History that occurred in 73 AD at the site in modern day Israel called Masada. *Masada Revisited* and *Masada Revisited II* contain more material of a historical and religious nature than *Masada Revisited III.* Book number six had title *Isaac and Amanda.* It is also about Isaac Newton and was also co-authored with Herbert Hauptman.